Nature's Voice

Health and Humanities

Nature's Voice

Health and Humanities

Professor Piero Formica

Edited and Preface by Aaron Greenberg

Foreword by Alan Barrell

Afterword by Brian Donnellan

bioGraph LLC
bioGraphbook.com

bioGraph LLC

Published by bioGraph
Chicago, IL
bioGraphbook.com

First bioGraph trade paperback edition December 2020

For information about discounts for bulk purchases,
please contact info@bioGraphbook.com

Cover Design by Guermandi Group
Manufactured in the United States of America
2 3 4 5 6 7 8 9 10

Printed on 90gsm acid-free paper

Library of Congress Control Number: 2021930019

ISBN: 978-1-951946-10-4 (paperback)

To Andrea Boltho and Fabrizio Galimberti,
companions of a long journey started in
Rue André Pascal, Paris, OECD headquarters.

Friendship projects the bright
ray of hope into the future

– *Cicero, Laelius on Friendship*

Another plague year would…bring us to see with differing eyes than those which we looked on things with before.

– Daniel Defoe, A Journal of the Plague Year, 1722

Nature humbled Ingram; it was his faith, and the nightingale's cry that evening reinforced his belief that nature's voice would always make itself heard, even at the darkest of times.

– Naoko Abe, "Cherry" Ingram: The Englishman Who Saved Japan's Blossoms, 2019

Human nature, you've been skilful, against yourself, and ingenious, in excess, to your own harm. What use to you are towns encircled with turreted walls? What use to you to add the discord of arms, at hand? When was the sea yours—land should have contented you! Why not seek out a third region then in the sky? Though you honour the sky too, Romulus, Bacchus, Hercules, Caesar now have temples. We dig the earth for solid gold not food.

– Ovid (43 BC - 17/18 AD), The Love Poems

CONTENTS

PREFACE

Aaron Greenberg, PhD

Researching for *Recorded Time: How to Write the Future,* bioGraph's memoir on the founding and origins of our business, I returned to an article saved from *Harvard Business Review*, where Professor Formica shows what entrepreneurs can learn from the model of Renaissance workshops, which put collaboration and knowledge at the center of value creation. As a Renaissance scholar turned entrepreneur, I was intrigued by Piero's insight into the innovation that describes bioGraph. With humility of creative ignorance, path creators reveal consumers' latent, unexpressed needs. We create new paths by accomodating humanity's storytelling nature, lest our narrative instinct stays stifled while we glorify and surrender data, neglecting our resources and obligation to co-author life with the voice of nature.

New technologies, in the full sense of *tékhne*, can make it easier and more productive than ever to understand, represent, and preserve our lives. Yet blind faith in data, biometrics, and social media lulls belief that stories of living memory and experience have been preserved, ready to access, practice, and re-create when time comes. However, with erudite industry and diligence resembling the ants honored in Bruno Latour's actor network theory, or further back like Aesop's ant, Professor Formica finds that if we ignore nature's voice, then infinite streams of data only clog the creativity whence innovation springs.

The internet tricks us to confuse facts and figures for cognition, mistaking data for knowledge, experience for wisdom. bioGraph was born from creative ignorance, which Piero discovers in artists, innovators, and entrepreneurs. We originated not from preconceived clients but to overcome our ignorance regarding life's data. Notwithstanding their etymology as that which is given, data are not given as indisputable facts. At our peril do we divorce data from the stories that shape and spring from them. "Data are useful," Formica writes, "but not if disconnected from the historical and cultural context depicted in narratives, which...are preferable to numbers when the physicality and hardness of measurements seems excessive." We tell stories to process experience and write the future. "Many are the roads that lead to the land of entrepreneurship where extraordinary phenomena occur," Piero professes. Naturally, given bioGraph's interdisciplinary entrepreneurialism and love for humanity, *Nature's Voice* called us.

Rediscovering Piero's *HBR* article, I introduced myself and thanked him for inspiration. The professor replied quickly from Bologna, Italy to book a virtual meeting. He wished me "salad days *à la* Shakespeare." This is the prime of youth when your judgment is green and you have invaluable zeal. Already well established with traditional publishers, Piero saw in bioGraph an empathic, agile, collaborative partner. "In this exceptional time in which we live," he wrote, "the work I propose must proceed as events unfold." Conventional publishing can be impersonal and ungainly. The timeliness of *Nature's Voice* needed diligent dispatch, speed as well as care, the sweet spot where bioGraph thrives.

The buzz around "data storytelling" reflects a truth that humans are storytelling animals who understand and shape the world through narrative. Without stories, we're left with cold facts on charts. There are more things in heaven and earth than are dreamt of via data. To those who hoard it, Formica asks: without narrative won't this feverish accumulation of data culminate in an undigested mass of numbers and information? "We can use narrative in tandem with the statistical, econometric, and probability models we already have," Piero writes, "but stories lift us beyond our current intellectual and creative limits."

Do we dare question data when there's epidemic distrust of "fake news" and contempt for experts, when public health is politicized, when we have whiplash from newfangled facts on the risks and benefits of this or that, open or closed, Remdesivir or Hydroxychloroquine, and so on *ad nauseam*? Piero argues not against data but against our misplaced trust and reliance on it at the expense of our storytelling nature. If we ignore data, we stick our heads in sand. Though if we overtrust it, then we forget Socrates' sooth, that wisdom is knowing we know nothing. Translating data into wisdom, stories teach us what we do not know. How, for instance, could we understand why some Black Americans and other minorities might suspect vaccines, if we don't know the shameful story of the Tuskegee Syphilis Study? And, had we not read *The Plague* (1947), could we recognize and regulate the incompetent human nature of authorities during epidemics? Camus writes,

> *...authorities still gave thought to propriety and it was only later that, by the force of things, this last remnant of decorum went by the board, and men and women were flung into the death-pits indiscriminately. Happily, this ultimate indignity synchronized with the plague's last ravages.*

Piero brightens the field of narrative medicine, whose torch is borne at institutions including Northwestern University Feinberg School of Medicine's Center for Bioethics and Medical Humanities, where I had the privilege of designing courses such as "A Long History of Longevity" and "What Therapeutic Misconception?" for medical students and residents. *Nature's Voice* argues for more humanities, hence more humanity, in healthcare. As the plague's fearful novelty waned, and the moving symbolism of nightly light shows honoring healthcare heroes went dark, many began to ignore reasonable pleas of those on the front lines of life and death. Nurses, doctors, and caregivers, paragons of *homo empathicus*, know there can be no health without humanity, having served as friends, family, spiritual guides, and more for strangers, hundreds of thousands dying isolated in the ICU. The least we can do is play our part, heeding nature's voice whether it calls through the buzzing of bees or epidemiology.

Like Walter Benjamin's ideal work as a collage of skillfully interwoven quotations, this book is a portable symposium where many voices converse with nature. What is the voice of nature? Is it Spinoza's *deus sive natura,* the Lucretian swerve, or Hobbes' war of all against all? This and more, nature's voice guides humanity while humbling human exceptionalism. Pandemics show that nature has life of its own, impassive to petty anthropomorphism and the socioeconomic *status quo*. Humans have been choking nature's voice at least since Ovid found us digging for gold. During the Renaissance, Reformation, empiricism, mechanism, and biopower midwived what's called the "death of nature." Piero finds nature alive, yet needing urgent care. *Nature's Voice* is both a warning and celebration. More than either hope or despair, it offers paths for humanity to thrive while preserving the nature that gives us life.

FOREWORD

Professor Alan Barrell

I have learned from experience not to approach any new book or treatise offered by Piero Formica without sufficient time to escape following protracted consideration and re-imagination stimulated by his deep and agile mind and the breadth of his ability to join up elements of life and existence that are too often divided through the conventions and constraints that capture us all. To be ourselves is difficult indeed. Artificial intelligence, so much discussed, and machine learning have yet to match the power of narrative and storytelling in causing many of us to re-examine our status and the prospects of our futures.

My words intend to persuade you to delve into this treasure trove of original thinking as you, like me, stagger and reel at this exhausting time of the ongoing pandemic. As I write, vaccines to deal with Covid-19 are just beginning to be delivered with much of human expectation of our generations hoping and willing, and praying if we believe in prayer, that this might be the beginning of the end. Piero, however, would have us believe that we have yet to arrive at the end of the beginning in ordering our minds to take account of how much has changed as the result of an organism some claim is not "living" in the sense of animal life as we generally consider it, cannot be seen or sensed in normal ways and has essentially thrown the world into disarray.

And, says Piero, what a time this is for us to re-imagine so much relating to the transdisciplinary bridges needed for human beings to find new ways of considering economics. How can human progress be evaluated following the shock in learning that GDP growth is not a given? Formica dares us to regard the context of our existence in the world, as one set of beings within an ecosystem so wondrous and complex that conventional "measurement" is meaningless beside the threat of unexpected disease and death about which we have been able to do so little.

Piero has ever been a stimulator for new thinking and new pathways. His references are many and likely to send us back to our bookshelves to revisit classic storytelling for new inspiration. Piero does not neglect the areas we have come to expect him to explore with new thoughts, such as entrepreneurship and entrepreneurialism. I am always drawn to deeper thinking by his references to "creative ignorance." As an octogenarian who spends most of life working with students from around the world of twenty years of age or little more, and loving every minute of it, I was struck by Piero's description of the young in this Covid and hopefully soon post-Covid world who are "swimming in the waters of doubt." In a sense, this treatise is a call to arms, and has made me consider the great importance of divergence and convergence: of culture, subject matter, technologies, art, and humanities. Connectedness, connectivity and "joined-upness" will surely be more important in the future than ever, but no less challenging. I end with a word, not yet in the dictionary, which I find myself using increasingly: "connectricity" or connectedness plus energy, one way we may rise to Piero's provocations and create the currents that determine the future.

Nature's Voice

Health and Humanities

THE STAGE SPACE

Nature's voice reaches us through bees and other pollinators. From them, we learn how to listen to and understand it. Yesterday's thinkers display the stage space by raising the curtain on tomorrow. Only the evolutionary surge in culture can enable humankind to surmount the constraints of economic and lifestyle models that have led to our failed relationship with nature.

Between 1961 and the present time, from the midst of post-World War II economic expansion to the globalisation of the 2000s, the human load on nature increased 2.5 times in terms of population and seven times when measured with GDP at constant prices. To the demographic and economic weight must be added the ponderousness of technology combined with hyper-specialisation. The race for quantity at the expense of quality extends to the limit of the biosphere, which under heavier burdens will no longer be able to sustain us. It is imperative to balance economic values with environmental concerns, to assess the compliance of human initiatives with the conservation of nature. It is equally vital to promote a generation of multifaceted thinkers and creators, polymaths familiar with different fields of study who have open minds to creatively resolve complex problems.

The voice of nature can be understood in the summer with the sound of bees buzzing, the abundant flowering of a variety of flower species, and flocks of birds circling in the sky. That voice tells us that most of the food we eat depends on pollinating insects. Owen Gaffney (2016), co-founder of Future Earth Media Lab, writes that "Almost 90% of wild plant species and over 75%

of crops we use for food depend in part on pollination by bees, butterflies and other animals."

It is estimated that the annual economic value of pollinators is in the range of $235-577 billion. Since 1961, the volume of agricultural production attributable to pollinators has increased by 300%. Even for coffee production, for which the roles of bees and other pollinators were deemed negligible, the pollination effect affects both the quantity, increasing it by about 10-20%, and quality, as demonstrated by the Global Coffee Report (2018). With large and growing portions of land destined to monoculture, the production of many crops drops and the habitat of pollinators impoverishes. In this way, bee species shrink at alarming rates, which weakens the voice of nature. Only by rediscovering the thread that binds cultural, agricultural, and biological diversity will it be likely to conceive healthy ecosystems that form the biosphere. In turn, the physical footprint of farms that practice intensification in agriculture would be erased.

With the curtain raised on today, it is through data that the voice of nature reaches the predominant commercial society. How much have the species of bees, butterflies, and tiny insects been reduced as a result of intensive farming, pesticide use, pollution, and climate change? How much damage do landslides cause to forests? How many more degrees of temperature will break records this summer? We are much more concerned about the value, for example, of our house built on the green lawn of a beautiful landscape than we care about the loss of bees. For those deaths, our interest stops at curiosity; it does not translate into action to safeguard the creatures of the ecosystem. We ask not how to save the bees, but rather how much the market value of our beautiful view will appreciate in the future.

Overindulging oneself, and thus conforming to harmful norms of commercial society, blinds us to the designs of nature's voice. We would not imagine the picture above as the best of all possible worlds. From Leibniz (1646-1716), we have to move towards Voltaire (1694-1778) and his *Candide* (1759) to realise that we are embedded in the living world whose diversity of interrelated organisms is startling. A legend tells that Ludwig van Beethoven (1770-1827) in search of inspiration used to wrap a large lime tree with his arms (Weiner, 2015). As John Stuart Mill (1806-1873) wrote *On Liberty* (1859),

> *Human nature is not a machine to be built after a model, and set to do exactly the work prescribed for it, but a tree, which requires to grow and develop itself on all sides, according to the tendency of the inward forces which make it a living thing.*

Neglecting conversation with nature to focus on whatever can bring personal gain, human beings have fought to hoard natural resources. Lack of collaboration towards a shared vision of resource allocation and environmental sustainability has narrowed the range of opportunities that nature offers humanity. We have forgotten, as Adam Smith (1723-1790) observed in his *Theory of Moral Sentiments* (1759), what nature has taught us, namely that "as the prosperity of two was preferable to that of one, that of many, or of all, must be infinitely more so."

Once we resume the thread of dialogue with nature, we will find that the stage space of the theatre where it is performed has been seized by HIV/AIDS, Ebola, SARS, MERS, Covid-19, and other pandemics that may become increasingly frequent. The alarms launched long ago went unheard. Almost half a century has passed since the French biologist Jean Rostand (1894-1977) voiced this in an interview with the Italian journalist Ugo Ronfani (1926-2009; 1972):

> *We biologists know that every attack against nature is also an attack against the human being, an attempt on his genetic patrimony. The most amazing technical discovery of these ten years is not worth the disappearance of a hundred species of animals... There is no progress if the balance between natural rhythms and scientific discoveries is not preserved.*

Health, claimed the philosopher Michel de Montaigne (1533-1592), "is a precious thing...without it, life is wearisome and injurious to us: pleasure, wisdom, learning, and virtue, without it, wither away and vanish." Will humankind, then, make good use of pandemics and diseases to become more resourceful? Will the future no longer be segregated into spaces that have proved to be virus-receptors and incubators of severe illnesses and existential disorders, spaces that the writer Simone de Beauvoir (1908-1986) called the Third World at home?

The philosopher Francis Bacon (1561-1626), the polymath Pierre-Simon Laplace (1749-1827) whose studies ranged from philosophy to physics and engineering, and the poet Giacomo Leopardi (1798-1837) showed humankind nature in the guise of a mechanism made of atoms under strict deterministic laws. A mechanism to be dominated because, as Leopardi maintained, nature is a stepmother who deceives her sons. In this pervasive intellectual atmosphere, the natural sciences and the human sciences have experienced detached lives. Following an opposite current of thought from Plato (428/427 BC - 348/347 BC) to the environmentalist James Lovelock (1919-), nature is a living organism, the realm of the born not of the made—a sort of great animal, according to the Greek philosopher—whose purpose is a planet suitable for life. In the crucible shaped by this vision, the fusion of all knowledge takes place. Original thoughts drawn from it lead to discoveries and works that facilitate its understanding and diffusion among the general public. Albert Einstein (1879-1955) said that reading the writings of the Scottish philosopher David Hume (1711-1776) helped him formulate the theory of special relativity. It is reported that Charles Darwin (1809-1882) considered the plant and landscape paintings of the botanical artist Marianne North (1830-1890) excellent examples of his theory of natural selection.

Stories crafted from the intellectual products of holistic knowledge are more than just anecdotes. The mixture of the sciences prompts collective action on the part of a variety of thinkers committed to tackling humanity's problems today. Facing nature, we witness the loss of biodiversity, climate change and the emergence of successive viral waves. In the field of international relations, increasing political uncertainty is fuelling nuclear tensions. Threats loom from asteroids that could impact the Earth's atmosphere. Amid a flood of adverse events, we are bewildered. We begin to realise that the emphasis on economics as a "hard" science, subservient to ever-increasing trade and consumption by individuals who aim solely at self-interest, has divorced humankind from nature.

(HOW) WILL SOCIETY CHANGE?

Once the curtain rises on the future, what will be the dominant scene that features reason and narrative as protagonists? Will we see a social landscape utterly different from the past?

In 2020, human beings, who had previously fled from nature, fell into its throat. How to get out of it? As in the Age of Enlightenment, will change make proselytes and marginalize those who fear it? In pursuit of innovation, advocates of change can turn to the power of reason rooted in accumulated knowledge. Alternatively or overlapping, they can rely on the power of narrative that stimulates and enriches the imagination. In order to practise innovation, the advocates of change will be able to resort to reason in the role of coach. Alternatively, they can rely on narratives. Between reason and narratives, the balance of the two forces is precarious.

"We must change" is the spirit of the time that moves reason to act. "Let us move because the others are moving": the change happens by analogy. Individually and in the social arena, one learns to innovate by drawing on research compiled by scientists and learning from ongoing experiments and then adapting one's behaviour and social customs to what has been assimilated. Such a learning process is exposed to the certainty mania syndrome, an antechamber of fanaticism, according to the French philosopher Ernest Renan (1823-1892). In his *Zibaldone*, the Italian poet Giacomo Leopardi (1798-1837; 2013) recalled the dictum of the

French philosopher Pierre Bayle (1647-1706): that reason is an instrument of destruction rather than construction. It sheds light on negative truths, on what in the more or less distant past was thought to be certain. This, however, does not mean that fallacies are no longer held as positive truths.

Strengthened by misinformation, people's tendency to reject new knowledge that contradicts beliefs lingers on. Within the boundaries of reason, long-established beliefs give distorting results and devastating outcomes. In the field of economics, the rule of profit maximisation is enlightening. As the economist Julie Nelson (2017) explains, companies that pursue this objective reduce their behaviour to a calculation, an operation that is not only conceivable and feasible but also mandatory. In the aura around the "sun" of compliance with the maximisation principle, productivity benefits obtained by farmers shift to their large suppliers and distributors. The merit of cultural products falls ruinously to the ground, having slipped on profitability and, therefore, on the number of buyers and views—all depending on the brand power of the companies doing business with cultural creations. An authoritative witness to both cases is the sociologist Zygmunt Bauman (1925-2017; 2005).

Narratives free us from the strings of knowledge that stifle the imagination as much as the dictatorial power of colonial dominions repressed the freedoms of subjugated populations. There are two ways to immerse oneself in a narrative. The first: read a certain number of pages day after day, until the end of the story. The second: continue living the ongoing story perpetually into the future, cultivating its rhizomatic possibilities.

Change is a moving target. Its trajectory is difficult to discern at first and only becomes apparent as the journey unfolds. The movement is smooth and fast. Entering the season of fantasy that opened with the crisis of Covid-19, imagination aroused by narrative will be the getaway from old ideas. Alas, this action is fraught with obstacles because, as John Maynard Keynes argued, the difficulty does not lie in new ideas, but in escaping from old ones. Those who must keep the "house in order" within the fence of accrued knowledge clash against the transformative power of storytellers, unreasonable people to draw new visions based on original values and beliefs.

The time of ecological crises is marked by the stories of the human species which, interacting with technology, interferes with nature. In the terrain of economics, agility and complexity of mind, combined with agile three-dimensional robots and 3D printers that can build complex things, are narrative themes that will point us in the direction of change as it progresses. By inventing our course, will we march differently from the past? Yes, once we grasp and master the irregularity of the landscape. The terrain comes into sight as a vast plain dotted with numerous holes of ignorance interrupted by hills of knowledge. Reason alone, which features wells of specialized knowledge, can do little to map and explore those holes.

We need transdisciplinarity that promotes encounters and integration of different knowledge maps, yielding innovative solutions, hybrid in nature and not attributable to a single, particular body of knowledge. Passion, imagination, and irrationality are prerequisites for this work. The Enlightenment, which emphasized the empire of reason, did not neglect them. Those who explore have the personality of the fox depicted by Isaiah Berlin (1909-1997; 1953) who developed into a parable a saying initially attributed to the Ancient Greek poet Archilochus (680 ca. 645 BC): "The fox knows many things, but the hedgehog knows one big thing." In the words of the philosopher and historian of ideas, those geographers and explorers pursue many ends, often unrelated and even contradictory, seizing upon the essence of accomplished experiences of a vast variety, compounded of heterogeneous elements.

THE NEW ERA

In the aftermath of the 2020 pandemic, new ideas and values have appeared on the horizon. The heart of the new era beats to the rhythm of an avant-garde of humanists—the "prosilients," proactive and resilient persons who rise up to see farther and further, and then jump and leap forward.

Steam technology triggered the industrial revolution and, later on, electrification favoured the progress of manufacturing technique. The intertwining of science, technology and the arts is the energy that has unleashed the knowledge revolution. Knowledge in action ("knowledgefication") is the energy source that ignites and moves immaterial values.

At the time of the steam engine, "Everything that is not a steam engine is a reverie" and humanity becomes "a mechanical species, which will necessarily act, in all circumstances, according to codified patterns of behaviour." So wrote Benjamin Constant (1767-1830), French political activist, to a cousin of his and, in the autumn of 1810, to the historian Prosper de Barante (1782-1866), according to the essayist Tzvetan Todorov (1939-2017; 1997).

Today returns us to that time. Is technology the absolute protagonist of our age? Solid empirical arguments can support the affirmative answer. However, the evidence is never definitive and irrevocable. Further investigations can steer in a completely different direction. Experience counts to a certain extent. For the philosopher Paul Feyerabend (1924-1994; 1978), retracing Aristotle's thought, experience "is what we perceive in normal circumstances in a normal environment and which we describe with words of everyday use." Extreme events drive the human being out of normalcy.

In the aftermath of the 2020 pandemic, new ideas and values have arisen on the horizon. Shadows to sweep away, according to the many who discern in the ground littered with revolutionary projects traps and obstacles to the customary way of life. Not scandals, but lights to follow for a minority that wants to proceed by finding, along the way, unusual fundamentals of life. To master knowledge, it is preferable to look inside oneself with the mind's eye. Intuition is of higher value than collecting information. That minority is composed of real people even before they are experts in a varied range of disciplines. Whether they are environmentalists, biologists, economists, engineers, or other professionals, they all share a strong creative and humanist spirit, not reduced to the realm of their interest.

The heart of the new era beats to the rhythm of avant-garde ideators, prosilient and versatile characters. Their knowledge is multiple and multi-faceted, associated with the ability to elevate, see further, and leap forward. Versatility and prosilience are habits of living in the certainty of uncertainty, entertaining the most varied scenarios and drawing actions to implement.

We will have the opportunity to recall several times the figure of the ideator who is central to the representation of an age in which, while nature calls into question the behaviour of human beings towards it, humans see their economic security threatened. To the "-" sign of job losses, the ideator contrasts the "+" sign of producing ideas. These, first of all, come from inside us. The ideator extracts them as David Hume (Rasmussen, 2017) would do, using ever more imagination and creativity, passion and wisdom. Unlike the young aristocrat Meno, Socrates' interlocutor, the ideator seeks what is unknown, even though he does not know what he must look for.

She is a storyteller of provisional truths that creates disorder, leaving listeners speechless. Numbers and graphs come later, because a bundle of facts and data is not knowledge, like a pile of stones is not a house: which the ideator learned from the French mathematician Henri Poincaré (1854-1912, 1902). The ideator activates the right part of the brain. For the left part, that of logic and rationality, computers may perform better than humans.

The ideator moves beyond the interaction of the two bits of intelligence, hers and the computer. The awareness of the strength expressed by the community to defend consolidated interests pushes the ideator to dialogue with the intelligence of small teams, intimate groups able to influence the behaviour of the community on a large scale. If new ideas are locked in a ghetto, their energy does not reach the general public. Those responsible for allocating resources in research and development would conform to the will of the majority. The intellectual exploration of the ideator would not bring about the change imagined as the innovation derived from the original thoughts would remain at the starting blocks. Therefore, the needed investments in health, environment, and education called for by the voice of nature would not be implemented. Such an outcome would leave the ideator disappointed and prostrate, who does not merely put her skills into practice but does so for a specific purpose. The aim is to listen to the voice of nature and to act accordingly to achieve a value proposition in contrast to the current trend with a few producers who make fortunes, while the number of low-paid workers swell and the voice of nature remains unheard.

NATURE AS PARTNER

Nature appears endowed with subjectivity and intelligence. If tomorrow must be designed with nature as a partner, not as an object, then in the discourse of design, the imagination of artists and the intellect of scientists must converse.

By acquiring knowledge, finding inspiration for discoveries, making them functional and, therefore applicable, *homo faber* pretended to be master of the world and lord of nature. With the appearance and development of communication networks, *homo communicator* thought that by operating in cyberspace for the unification between the forces of atoms (machines) and the forces of bits (information) it was feasible to accelerate the process of subjecting nature to human will. In light of climate change and pandemic events, nature appears endowed with subjectivity and intelligence, as the poet Titus Lucretius Caro (94 B.C.-50 or 55 B.C.) maintained. Nature is not an object to be conquered and dominated. For Goethe, "Nature is living, [it is not] pure quantity....game to be captured...a tool to be forged according to the usefulness of man" (Goethe, 2020). With the message "nothing can be as it was before," Covid-19 showed humanity in a state of hominescence, as the philosopher Michel Serres (1930-2019) would say. We are all adolescents and, therefore, in a continuous change that occurs on the threshold of something unpredictable (Serres, 2001; Bellusci, 2016).

The transition from adolescence to adulthood is rough. Guided by Montaigne (1993), we may say with Horace: *Ducimur ut nervis alienis mobile lignum* ("We are guided like the wooden puppet, moved by the muscles of others." – *Satyrae*, II, VIIII); that is, the muscles of unknown viruses. Sheltering from sickness, in a backroom of our own, we face a unique challenge: *In solis sis tibi turba locis* ("In solitude, be company for thyself." – *Tibullus, Elegiae*, IV, VIII, 12). As Montaigne writes, (1993): "We have a mind pliable in itself, that will be company; that has wherewithal to attack and to defend, to receive and to give: let us not then fear in this solitude to languish under an uncomfortable vacuity." Called to plan tomorrow, to the obsession of wanting to be always right we prefer modesty that leads to accepting reversals of course, because: *Malum consilium est, quod mutari non potest* ("It is evil counsel that will admit no change." – *Publilius Syrus*, quoted by Aulus Gellius, *Noctes Atticae*, XVII, 14). We might also muse with another philosopher, Giovanni Papini (1881-1956; 1906), who wonders: "Is a project not the tea, the coffee, the opium, the hashish of life? Is it not the substitute, the surrogate, the down-payment of reality?"

Should tomorrow be designed with nature as a partner, not as an object, then in the discourse of design we will find the imagination of artists and the intellect of scientists conversing. Artists do not erase the past; they look to their predecessors. The poet, writer and playwright Johann Wolfgang von Goethe (1749-1832) was one of the masters from whom artists learned how to participate in the vital impulse of nature: art acting in the guise of nature. Conversely, scientific minds prone to nature ought to get rid of attractive forces exerted by a past when the environment was configured as an asset to be exploited. Traditional knowledge bearing such an approach to nature is excessively heavy and dangerous baggage for those whom the scientist Galileo Galilei (1564-1642) named "doctors of memory." The intellect cannot travel to the future with its shoulders turned backwards and loaded with that weight. With such behaviour, it takes so long to lose sight of the objective of advancing knowledge by intervening on the uneven balance of power between material progress and nature. Rebalancing the relationship in support of the latter is a task for designers at the crossroads of art and science. They are "creative ignoramuses" who, as the philosopher and mathematician René Descartes (1596-1650) would say, can judge "with much greater solidity and clarity." They are outsiders—that is, non-experts who, not knowing a subject, tackle it from a totally different angle than the seasoned experts who know it thoroughly (Formica, 2015).

CONVERSING WITH NATURE

In turbulent waters of natural events, conversation prevents drowning under the weight of many given interpretations. In conversation's gymnasium, social exchange of thoughts begets empathy. The words that collide give life to new, original words that sweep away many trivial debates and rituals.

Nature is an artist. One of her most seductive works is the spring blossoming of Japanese cherry trees. Hanami, the custom of admiring the beauty of their blossoming, takes us on a journey with imagination to where there is no path yet. We have much to learn from nature's economy. With the language of Japanese cherry trees, it speaks to us of the diversity of species and varieties of knowing how to approach and hybridise them. Diversity is the remedy to asphyxiating the homogeneity that hinders human progress.

Conversing about nature is the equivalent of dancing to the rhythm of a harmonious concert of instruments. Conversation, however, does not ape harmony; it is not conformism. If pollution impairs the beauty of nature, social and political practices strongly imbued with conformism destroy its identity, which manifests itself in the multiplicity of its species. Japanese cherry trees know it well, at their expense. In Japan, willingly secluded from the rest of the world, many species of cherry blossom trees, emblem of the character of the land of the Rising Sun, were marginalised. Nature suffered. In the 1880s, 30% were Somei-yoshino cherry. In her history of Japanese ornamental cherry trees, the writer Naoko Abe (2019) recalls that at the time of her childhood, in the early 1960s, seven out of ten were of that variety, a number that "spoke volumes about the dark path of conformity which the Japanese followed, until their 1945 defeat."

Conversation does not lead in the direction of the pre-traced path. It goes where there is no path yet. There is, therefore, discomfort, restlessness and bewilderment in conversation, but the air of conversation is clean. The dust accumulates when varieties of ideas expressed become fragments so tiny as to make them indistinguishable. To avoid uniformity due to conformism, it would be wise, sometimes, to put one's well-ordered head at rest on the pillow of ignorance, as Montaigne would say, and then wake up with singular curiosities.

The willingness to grow with an ever-increasing trade cannot ignore the protection of the natural environment, the charm of landscapes that nature has so generously bestowed on us. A walk in the woods, the sound of a waterfall, and the spring bloom of Japanese cherry trees are sources of inspiration. Arranging roads, avenues, and parks with these trees would secure a sign of human commitment to care for nature's economy. Looking at their spring blossoming would instill hope in the future and preserve the memory of the dead during the plague. A community of citizens in solidarity with nature can transplant and cultivate flowering cherry trees in their territory. Naoko Abe reminds us that "nature's voice would always make itself heard, even at the darkest of times." Planting Japanese cherry trees in our backyard is a special way to listen to nature's voice.

Being together (from the Latin *conversari*) is the art of imagination, exploration, experimentation, and creation, in a dynamic balance between introspection and open-mindedness, which touches the most sensitive strings of human invention projected towards the future. We converse by interacting and listening deeply to build trust, understanding and, therefore, harmonious relationships. We converse to improve and unite, according to that great conversationalist and "nation-builder" Benjamin Franklin (1706-1790). He argued that "the chief ends of conversation are to inform or to be informed, to please or to persuade" by adopting the Socratic method of the "humble inquirer and doubter," and, therefore, "drop[ping] abrupt contradiction and positive argumentation."

Conversation demands thinkers, ideators who shun the pedantry of experts. These, to return to Montaigne, spread their books and words everywhere, creating a vortex of exegesis and interpretations. The swarming of reciprocal comments, altercations, and excessive attachment to forms overwhelms and suffocates the listener. Otherwise, the interlocutor can freely enter distant cognitive territories. The naturalist Charles Darwin (1809-1882) rode the wave of the economist Thomas Malthus (1766-1834) in elaborating the theory of evolution—and collaborated to eliminate the background noise of colliding ideas. So acting, during the conversation, intercepted signals reveal solutions to problems under discussion. Transmission and expansion of knowledge through conversation enhance each other's intelligence, leading to discoveries such as that of the structure of the DNA molecule, which earned the biologists Francis Crick (1916-2004) and James Watson the Nobel Prize for Medicine in 1962.

NATURE AND GDP

Human actions should be in tune with the nature that sustains life on Earth. We are witnesses and protagonists of the birth of a new universe in whose economic galaxy not all revolves around the Gross Domestic Product.

There is the world of nature, of all that is born. Paul Klee (1879-1940), a painter and, first and foremost, a naturally gifted draughtsman who mastered the theory of colours, cultivated a desire to plunge into nature, to be at one with the natural world. On the occasion of the 1923 Bauhaus exhibition, he told his students and wrote in the *Ways to Study Nature* that "The artist is a human being, himself nature and a part in the realm of nature" (Crevel, 1930; Klee, 2013). Then there is the world we make, the kingdom of human makings whose economic performance can be recounted in the Gross Domestic Product.

In the prism of relationships between nature and GDP, the patrimony of human behaviour shines light from two primary sources. Drawing from the tradition of Aesop's "The Grasshopper and the Ant" (620 B.C-564 B.C), the one source is the Ant's solicitous, industrious, and frugal habit; the other, the Grasshopper's inspired light-heartedness. In the GDP of ants, a variety of goods so attractive to Grasshoppers stands out. In the GDP of the latter, there are plenty of houses, hotels, shopping malls, parks, and amusement places by the sea that appeal to ants, eager to escape the cold wind that blows and ready to accept the beguiling invitation of the sun's rays in the countries of the Grasshoppers. With the large amount of money that comes from the purchases of the Ants, the Grasshoppers can resort to more bank loans, even from banks and customers of the frugal country, loans supported by land prices that speculation only inflates.

In the unravelling of the age of knowledge, nature and humanity mutually attract. Life merges with digital intelligence. Machines have visual perception; recognizing spoken and written words, they translate from one language to another. On the other hand, technology, especially bioengineering, interferes with human nature. What connects and engages the two worlds are the ideas that spread, evolve, and mutate like living organisms. Dialoguing with nature, the poet draws ideas from imagination. Scientists test them. For ideas that go viral, evolutionary biologist Richard Dawkins coined the term "meme," analogue to the "gene." The faster the media, the more rapidly spread the memes.

Assuming that the "born" and the "made" endowed with different characteristics tend to converge, this does not guarantee their concordance. Actions in the "realm of made" should be in tune with nature's efforts to ensure that the planet Earth is life-worthy. It is not so, for the thought that this convergence is only a different point of view prevails. On the contrary, we are witnesses and protagonists of the birth of a new universe in whose economic galaxy not everything revolves around Gross Domestic Product (GDP). Social scientists identify GDP as a major obstacle to concordance. An artefact designed to measure the economic value of production, the "calf" GDP in the 1930s has long been a "bull" whose posture is furious and tyrannical. With the "+" sign next to the sum of market operations that make up the GDP, governments remain firm on their feet; with the "-" sign, they fall. Those operations depend on the commitment of the productive forces, identified with land, labour and capital—a task which still results, as a legacy of bygone times, in physical fatigue.

The concordance would require policymakers to downgrade GDP from its pre-eminence. Its hegemony is undeserved, according to Angus Deaton, winner of the 2015 Nobel Memorial Prize in Economic Sciences, if GDP is "interpreted as a measure of how well the economy is serving its people." Other heavenly bodies—the indexes of happiness (Gross National Happiness), human development (Human Development Index) and progress (Genuine Progress Indicator), and data on poverty—also exist in the galaxy. The gravitational force between all these bodies is the subject of extensive and heated debate. According to Deaton (2020), the GDP accounting can be perfected by

> *excluding many of the things that do not improve human well-being (like useless but profitable medical procedures), and ensuring a much better account of distribution—in particular, how personal disposable income is distributed among different groups.*

Besides, the contribution of assets such as research and development, innovative capabilities, software, human capital, social relations, cultural values, and benevolence must be assessed with extreme care. These intangible values increase productivity and instigate innovation.

Cultural changes would restore nature to its due rank. For quality of life, from public health to climate, drastic policies to combat air pollution could be implemented, using green charges such as carbon taxes and limits on land and air traffic. Environmental sustainability would regulate the mobility flows of both people and goods. Accordingly, investments should be directed towards the restoration of degraded land, sanitisation, environmentally friendly transport and unconventional energy—a set of actions to achieve a more resilient economy. With the GDP as a conventional unit of measurement, its dogmatic advocates have the green light to oppose those policies. The cost burden of renewable and unconventional energy sources and the collapse of significant parts of the traditional economy would shrink resources for environmental protection. Yet, the pursuit of the common good has a vital role to play in helping to counter these arguments, as we shall see shortly.

DESIGNERS AND FORECASTERS

Nature's partner is the designer who looks forward to shaping the future together with nature. It is not the forecaster who focuses entirely on past events and then anticipates how the present flows into the future.

The year 2020 will be remembered for human health returning as the main character in the theatre where the daily experience of climate change, bioterrorism, cyberattacks, and misuse of artificial intelligence, to name but a few realistic threats, take the stage. By early 2020, humanity had lost its way. The World Bank, in its Global Economic Prospects report, made the following statement:

> *Covid-19 is the most adverse peacetime shock to the global economy in a century. This is forecast to be the fourth-worst global recession since 1871. Never since 1871 has such a high proportion of economies [over 90%] been in recession.*

Under the attack of the invisible killer Covid-19, the trailblazers who create new paths along which our material life travels exhibited a variety of scenarios. The V-shaped scenario shows the economy heading back to the growth path before the virus attack and then, perhaps, taking another path that can be travelled at an even faster pace. Laurence Boone, Chief Economist of the

OECD, in the June 2020 Economic Outlook, raised doubt about this vision:

> *Most people see a V-shaped recovery, but we think it is going to stop halfway. By the end of 2021, the loss of income exceeds that of any previous recession over the last 100 years outside wartime, with dire and long-lasting consequences for people, firms and governments.*

In the U-shaped scenario, the previous speed is resumed but the gap to be filled remains wide. This means a one-time event of economic loss. In the L-shaped scenario, the loss of productive activity is continuously increasing because it slows the economy's pace of growth. Michael Spence, winner of the 2001 Nobel Memorial Prize in Economic Sciences, and Chen Long (2020) have designed a scenario involving an S-shaped recovery. The acceleration would be slow but steady. However, close to pre-pandemic production levels, the sectors that will face the hardest difficulties due to persistent social distancing would decelerate the pace of recovery. According to the economist Nouriel Roubini (2020), the fifth scenario, I-shaped, is a vertical line outlining the real economy and financial markets in a free-fall. In the *Financial Times* of June 10, 2020, economist Peter Atwater designed a K-shaped path, with the gap widening. On the one hand, rebounded confidence between most of the world's largest companies, the rich, and people working at home; on the other, conditions further worsened for small businesses, the working class, and many workers in essential roles.

On March 11, 2020, the Director-General of the World Health Organization stated, "We have assessed that Covid-19 can be characterized as a pandemic." From that day on, anyone looking at the scene where health is the main protagonist sees three supporting players in action. Two are designers: one visionary, the other pragmatic. The third is an economic forecaster. Their actions to confront the virus reveal three different social identities that denote their respective communities. Leaving the past behind, the two designers look forward, downstream, to prepare for the future. Conversely, the forecaster's commitment is entirely focused on upstream events and assumes how the present flows into the future. The visionary designer directs the compass towards medical research to yield results so innovative and with an unprecedented speed that lives can be saved while preventing economic misery, thus propelling the economy's V-shaped recovery. This is the direction taken by the Bill & Melinda Gates Foundation, together with Wellcome and Mastercard, who announced on March 10, 2020 an initiative to accelerate development and access to treatment. "Covid-19 Therapeutics Accelerator," reads the press release, "will coordinate R&D efforts and remove barriers to drug development and scale-up to address the epidemic."

The pragmatic designer would also encourage a V-shaped recovery, innovating to incrementally enhance innovation while extending its scope. She broadens the view, turning her attention to all who can pioneer new ways of exploiting innovation. Starting with virtual reality (VR), augmented reality (AR), and artificial intelligence (AI) to create "healthy homes for healthy people," since 2018 the Californian entrepreneur Sheridan Tatsuno has been working to extend energy, temperature, and traffic monitoring programmes in cities to healthcare. In collaboration with the medical world, Tatsuno designs to apply the VR models, developed by his company One Reality to protect the environment, combat climate change, and monitor patients with COPD (chronic obstructive pulmonary disease), the third leading cause of death in the United States. With VR devices, diagnoses could be faster and cheaper.

The forecasting expert causes undesirable or unintended effects in the economic environment. She does not feel called upon to remedy the shortcomings of the past, which compels her to dismiss revolutionary ideas and to nurture many doubts about incremental concepts. The former would require a waste of resources over indefinitely long periods. The latter take time to materialise. Better, then, the forecaster thinks, to rely on mature ideas and accelerate their spread. Going backwards, for example, to the nineteenth century, the forecaster prefers the anaesthetic that solves the immediate pain over the antiseptic that protects against the invisible and delayed attack of infection. What is immediately perceived is incorrectly deemed appropriate.

The context of thought changes passing from visionaries to pragmatists and forecasters. At one extreme, there are visionaries whose vision is innate. As Sigmund Freud (1856-1939) would say, they seize on the pleasure principle which unleashes their imaginative energy and makes them find the unpredictable. The Sicilian writer Leonardo Sciascia (1921-1989; 1975) refers us to the paradigmatic figures of Filippo Brunelleschi (1377-1446), the visionary architect of the dome of Santa Maria del Fiore in Florence, and the theoretical physicist Ettore Majorana (1906 and missed in 1938) whose studies on neutrino opened new frontiers in physics. At the other extreme, we find the forecasters who, discarding the pleasure principle, tend towards the reality principle. They are conditioned by the state of experiential knowledge and habits of thought prevailing in their communities. The pragmatic designer disciplines the impulse between pleasure and reality by descending into the arena of research and innovation with great will power that compensates for the absence of natural talent.

Did human health come into the picture because it was suddenly pushed there by Covid-19? Or should we have been prepared for the event by listening to alarms raised by previous epidemic events? In one case and another, naked on stage, health created considerable unease among the realists. The pleasure principle and the reality principle are imbalanced, with huge repercussions for humanity. The latter's excessive weight prevents the joyful liberation of imagination, enticer of visionary discoveries. The popular sentiment is an enormous boulder. Have we lost our way? Well, let us try to find it by all means. Woe to turn back and seek routes in new directions. It is on the road familiar to us that, after all, we have staked our lives. To get it back, we will never give up. As Robert Short (1932-2009; 1968) reminds us, the poet Thomas Eliot (1888-1965; 1951) called this obstinacy supported by so much application "a necessary move / In an unnecessary action [which] Not for the good it will do / But that nothing may be left undone On the margin of the impossible."

To take a completely different course of action, we would have to bring down economic growth from the scale. By stepping on it, economic growth watches its weight increase. What matters is quantity. After the pandemic outburst, a V-shaped recovery is a quick climb. At the end of July 2020, updating the March forecast, Nouriel Roubini (2020) wrote,

> *After falling by 30-40% at the beginning of the pandemic, many equity markets have recovered most of their losses, owing to the massive fiscal-policy response and hopes for an imminent Covid-19 vaccine. The V-shaped recovery in markets indicates that investors are anticipating a V-shaped recovery in the economy.*

In the same month, another economist, Jim O'Neill (2020), claimed that "If a V-shaped recovery does arrive, it will be important to shift attention to other issues, such as the quality of future growth." The Latin word for climbing is *scandere*, from which we get "scale." Scalability has obsessed economists. To increase the scale of production, that is, to enlarge the size of the enterprise, the production unit or the plant, involves reducing the average unit cost of the product, an unmissable economic advantage. The "scale principle" is eternal and universal. In the Paleolithic Age, Ronald Wright (2004) observes, killing two mammoths instead of one was considered progress; progress so notable that it was excessive and, therefore, harmful because the hunters ended up starving to death. Much later in time, with the succession of waves of industrialization, that principle extended from industry to services and agriculture. Today, industrial farms devote themselves to a single crop covering thousands of acres. Donna Kilpatrick (2020), who chairs Heifer Ranch, an American agricultural training facility, has made a regenerative proposal for agriculture: "By diversifying crops, farmers can better withstand crises and protect and promote healthy agricultural ecosystems."

By scaling, we want to ascend to the realm of quantity, where everything susceptible to increase or decrease can be measured. From the scale, however, we fall if we neglect quality, not as a byword for luxury but the well-being of humanity and nature. Let's recall the remark attributed to Goethe: "There is a big shadow where there is much light." Germany is Europe's engine and a global economic power, as its brands have mastered quality mass production. Does this quality account for the price of non-compliance with nature? The sooner we intervene, the closer we get to restoring equilibrium between humanity and nature, a balance which today is heavily weighted in favour of the former.

HUMAN STORYTELLER

The world of facts no longer provides reassurances it once did. Nowadays, it feels like facts have many meanings, and those facts are fleeting. Shall we long for the old certainties? Or should we, instead, find stories and narratives that help us make sense of our own insecure, unsteady position? By sailing in the hot air balloon of narratives, facts and data rise to a higher reality.

The hardship of the time in which we are living puts human creativity to the test. Rather than succumbing to despair, one must let oneself be seized by the wonder that the German sociologist Max Weber (1864-1920) called "the capacity to be amazed." Without such wonder and amazement, human beings merely solve existing problems, and computers can do that better than we can. Disorder and uncertainty are an invitation and a challenge to our minds. We must get rid of existing questions and uncover new ones; those new questions will spur us to work out radical solutions to the threats we face. To identify problems and then solve them, we need to look for other pathways: those stemming from narratives, stories, and conversations. We can use narrative in tandem with the statistical, econometric, and probability models we already have. But stories lift us beyond our current intellectual and creative limits.

Hard-headed economists and scientists might shudder to admit it, but this is nothing new. Literature has always been the muse of the economy. Fairy tales, fables, stories, novels, and essays arouse emotions and ideas that affect economic activity. Through books, diverse species of ideas come into contact. Their pollination produces entirely new ideas, provided that the book can be peeled. One has to get inside the book, in that treasured part under the "peel." The Latin word for book is *liber*, which also means the inner part of the bark of the tree, precious because it is white and therefore suitable for writing on. It is not enough to know how to read and write. We must learn, unlearn and apply what we learn: an exercise that entails the imagination born from reading the text as well as interacting with the author, the publisher, and other readers. The conversation takes place both verbally and through the circulation of our notes in the book. Annotating a text, commenting in the margin, and reproducing with signs real or imagined things: these are the marginalia that readers over the centuries have produced for purposes sometimes personal, sometimes to enlarge their scope from private to social reading. The book, therefore, stretches beyond boundaries drawn by the author to penetrate the vast territories of readers' imagination where extraordinary works of thought can arise.

Literature inspires reform, including of human behaviour, to counter "the mind and the heart terribly corrupt," as Madame de La Fayette (1634-1693), the advocate of the ideal of sociability, would have wished. Literature encourages us to recognize and accept other people; it allows us to understand their minds and motivations. Reading stories, we develop open minds and understanding of others. In turn, this inspires spontaneous social connections and sympathies without the heavy-handed intervention of the law. The study of literature and other art forms also has immediate and practical benefits for economic activity. It can promote communication, analytical thinking, and precision of expression, allowing one to embrace uncertainty and imperfection.

Most importantly, reading stories frees the imagination, inspiring new ways of seeing, new ways of thinking. Literary conversations are non-linear. In creative environments, we give and receive ideas freely. The free exchange of ideas, beyond any material or economic considerations, forged the most fertile creative environments in human history: the symposiums in Athens, the artistic workshops of Medici Florence, the salons of the French dames of the seventeenth and eighteenth centuries, Benjamin Franklin's Junto Club in Philadelphia, the English clubs that were the hotbeds of the first industrial revolution, and the Adda that shaped the Bengal Renaissance.

In Plato's *Symposium*, for example, Socrates and his friends stay up late discussing love and desire. The air is festive; some have been up for days, carousing, attending tragedies, debating the contours of a good life. The conversation is democratic. Rather than simply having Socrates lecture his friends, they all get their say. This shows it is better to provide a range of pathways, narratives, and stories rather than to insist on one viewpoint. In its branching possibilities, the *Symposium* encourages us to think open-mindedly to find our own path through the thickets of desire.

Modern quantitative experiments support Plato's intuition. MIT professor Alex Pentland has shown that water-cooler conversations among colleagues are not a waste of time, though they might appear so to anxious managers: "One team was given a shared coffee break, while the other, efficiently, staggered theirs, so work was uninterrupted. The social team's job satisfaction went up, and it was $10m more profitable. What's happening in that wasted time? People were sharing information, problem-solving, motivating and helping one another" (Heffernan, 2020). Conversation, while inefficient, democratic, and hard to quantify, is key to solving problems in business and economics. Without such freedom of exchange, people fall into the same ruts, the tried and tired ideas. Companies that employ them suffer as a result. In the social sciences, too, researchers are turning their attention to narrative, arguing that stories can substantially shape human behavior. People are not always rational actors. Their response to a crisis may not be driven by clear-eyed analysis of the facts. Instead, it may come from panic or ignorance; it may be determined by the stories circulating in the media. As Robert Shiller (2017), recipient of the 2013 Nobel Memorial Prize in Economic Sciences, writes,

> *We have to consider the possibility that sometimes the dominant reason why a recession is severe is related to the prevalence and vividness of certain stories, not the purely economic feedback or multipliers that economists love to model.*

The aristocrats of data dream of embarking for the island of incontrovertible facts and, once there, they would organize a gallant party in honor of those facts. Jean-Antoine Watteau (1684-1721) gives us a vivid image of what such a festival might look like in *The Embarkation for Cythera* (1717): the small-minded and self-satisfied out for a weekend pleasure cruise, with fat little putti doing cartwheels in the sky. It's a seductive vision, but a false one: we must always remember that Cythera—Aphrodite's island, the seat of unimaginable pleasure—is the destination of our earthly journey. But it is not attainable by mere mortals. So too, the island of incontrovertible facts is our goal, but only the foolhardy imagine they will arrive there. Solid empirical arguments are never definitive and irrevocable. Further investigations can steer us in a completely new direction. The Baconian scientific method requires one to reach the sacred shore of reality by standing on the stable boat of facts. But, in pursuit of the facts, the boat is constantly obliged to retreat and change directions. To love facts is to love polygamously: to love many things and ideas, subject to contradictory and ever-changing winds. The journey continues. Its unfolding is a story of misadventure and happenstance, chance encounters and felicitous accidents. It involves the protagonistic scientists and economists who search so vigorously for truth, and those they meet on the way, observers of their quest whose behaviour is affected by what they learn from conversing with these truth seekers. The shore of reality has a narrative form: it is the story we tell ourselves about our search for truth.

By admitting that stories are key to scientific and economic progress, will we get a clearer view of the disruptive events that have seized our society? A scientist might insist that the best way to respond is to accumulate as much data as possible. But without a narrative to make sense of the data, won't this obsessive, feverish search end in an overwhelming and undigested mass of numbers and figures? In his story, "On Exactitude in Science," Jorge Luis Borges (1889-1986; 1998), the Argentine fabulist, imagines a society that has indulged, to a dangerous degree, in gathering data for its own sake:

> *In that Empire, the Art of Cartography attained such Perfection that the map of a single Province occupied the entirety of a City, and the map of the Empire, the entirety of a Province. In time, those Unconscionable Maps no longer satisfied, and the Cartographers Guilds struck a Map of the Empire whose size was that of the Empire, and which coincided point for point with it.*

As Nobel Prize Winner Richard P. Feynman (1918-1988) remarks in *The Uncertainty of Science*, "It is not always a good idea to be too precise." Otherwise, one arrives at a map as big as the thing it maps: perfectly accurate and perfectly useless. Only a narrative, a story, can balance between accuracy and imprecision. Without such a balance, science fails.

To seek data, to get access, and then to count and describe them, is a sterile exercise if not underpinned by an interpretive theory. Vision draws nourishment from ideas born of pure fantasy as well as from the human capacity to intuit and anticipate reality. It is the narration of mental operations, from the collection of data to their interpretation, that gives completeness to knowing. Its ultimate goal, however, is not the illustration of vision, but the impact it will have on society. The story must be spread to be known and compared with others. From the narratives we intersect, new and more advanced visions mature.

To defeat viruses, to break the chain of transmission of diffusive and contagious infections, we must learn from events such as that of Ignaz Semmelweis (1818-1865), who in 1847 discovered how much childbirth fever resulted from lack of handwashing in maternity wards. At that time, that idea was considered subversive. The resistence it faced came from dearth of narrative communication. Referring to hardships endured by that Hungarian doctor as told by Sherwin Nuland (2003) in *The Doctor's Plague*, Greg Satel (2019) commented: "Semmelweis didn't see the value in communicating his work effectively, formatting his publications clearly or even collecting data in a manner that would gain his ideas greater acceptance."

In a world of facts with many elusive meanings, we need storytelling's connective tissue. It not only facilitates an encounter between scientists and artists. It also connects the facts of the laboratory and the truths of the novel, the reality of the empirical study and the experience of the person who must live in the reality which that study seeks to describe. Stories give the flexibility and freedom of mind we need, lest the pomp and pretence of science overwhelm us. When we see the City of Facts in the mists, we are not blinded by its splendour: the stories we tell act like sunglasses that protect our eyes. Our narratives allow us to see facts more clearly, in greater detail. The City of Facts is not the Emerald City where the Great and Terrible Wizard of Oz reigns, and which one must enter with green-tinted spectacles to protect oneself from the brightness. If we were all forced to use the same stories, wear the same sunglasses, reality itself would be reduced to a drab conformity, its pleasure and possibility dissolved.

As we confront the global crisis induced by Covid-19, we must be willing to recognize that outmoded ways of thinking have failed and that new stories are needed to grasp and represent our new reality. What better time to review and revise the facts, to see them with new eyes and invent ways of reckoning with them? What better time to interrogate assumptions of scientists and economists? The time is now to repair the connective tissue between disciplines that have been unnaturally torn. Now, as ever, is time to tell stories.

NARRATIVE MEDICINE

As for the universe, so for the human body: most of it is invisible to normal light. Narrative is a glow that illuminates parts of the body in shadow, for it casts so much light on the personalities of those inhabiting it. A transdisciplinary habitat addressed to narrative medicine is a life project for those responsible for their health and seeking nature's welfare for their own.

The most frequent answers to the growing demand for healthcare lie in technology. Smart policies must ensure that innovations do not alienate humanity from medicine and thereby drive patients away from doctors. Personal attention, the encounter between healthcare professionals and patients, is a precious resource in technological medicine.

In the wake of the global health emergency midwifed by Covid-19, the Italian Society of Narrative Medicine (SIMeN) has designed R-ESISTERE (www.resistere.medicinanarrativa.it), a collective memory platform built by sharing stories, experiences, and snapshots of reality. Since it is human behaviour that makes the difference, the platform "gathers the stories of illness, treatment, healing or, sadly, death, but sometimes also simple everyday life, of those who have lived and are living the experience of the pandemic." SIMeN maintains,

Narrative Medicine is a methodology of clinical-assistance intervention grounded on a specific communicative competence, with areas of application in clinics, training and research. The narrative is an invaluable tool to capture, understand, and

integrate the different points of view of those who intervene in the disease and the treatment process in order to achieve the shared construction of a customised care path.

Healthcare and socio-medical operators, elaborating analyses and comments of personal stories, will gain greater awareness of their professional role and of the emotional world that surrounds them. People will eschew the patient's robes and transform themselves with their stories into protagonists of the care process.

From this perspective, one can infer the decisive role that universities should play in forging links between humanities, on the one hand, and medicine on the other. The past happens to point the way to the future. In the seventeenth century, outstanding figures such as Marcello Malpighi (1628-1694), pioneer of microscopy, who studied medicine and philosophy at the University of Bologna, and Edward Tyson (1651-1708), scholar of the relationship between man and animals, who graduated in literature at Oxford and medicine at Cambridge, stand out.

The infrastructure to be built is a transdisciplinary habitat designed for narrative medicine. Here we are met by Rita Charon, internist and Henry James (1843-1916) scholar at Columbia University Irving Medical Center in New York. Charon has been working on this issue for more than two decades and has proven which kind of listening doctors can give patients by drawing from literature and the arts and then writing, drawing, and sharing their stories of clinical encounters.

By crossing the bridge linking the humanities and liberal arts, on one side, and medicine, on the other, young people would be increasingly aware of innovative careers in health. Medical issues will be intertwining with sensibilities arising from literary culture and artistic creativity for a better understanding of medicine's socioeconomic, cultural, political, and ethical implications.

Writers the likes of Cronin and Tobino reveal how narrative addresses the gap in performance provided by data and facts. A.J. Cronin (1896-1981), an English writer and physician, was a masterful narrator of ethical issues looming for those embarking on the medical profession. How should a healthcare professional who sees his innovative methods of treatment met with hostility, first, by his colleagues, behave? Andrew Mason, the protagonist of *The Citadel* (1937), Cronin's revolutionary novel centred on medical ethics, resolves to resign from his position. An abandonment of ethics ensues. Mason is attracted by easy gains he makes by joining a chain of favours between fashionable surgeons and wealthy, spoiled patients. Enriched, then involved in the death of a sick man, he returns to his path littered with progressive ideas, practising his profession in a small community in the West Midlands.

Such behavioural cycles are conducive to literary interests. But amid a crowd of numbers used to collect statistical data to convert into facts, stories *à la* Mason are lost in anonymity. In the narrative field of innovation, one enters with a restless and evasive anxiety about the uncertain first step to be taken. Such a disposition reinforces with innovation linked to ethical choices, as when Mason faced the obscurantism of university teaching, mistrust mixed with ignorance and arrogance of colleagues, the habit of resorting to useless and harmful practices, and people's aversion to innovative methods of treatment.

Mario Tobino (1910-1991), an Italian writer and psychiatrist, turns his working life at the asylum in Magliano into stories. From *The Mad Women of Magliano* (1954) to *Gli Ultimi Giorni di Magliano* (1982), his narratives give value and meaning unparalleled in the data and facts on the evolution of psychiatry in Italy. It unfolds from pre-pharmacology with the imprisonment of the sick in asylums, to pharmacology with the experimentation of the first drugs and, later, the anti-psychiatry that closes psychiatric hospitals. Tobino asks where to take care of patients once those hospitals are closed. Without alternative solutions, evolutionary innovation hangs on nothing. His narration brings on stage one of the most controversial disputes about innovation: namely, the interfaces between its applications and their consequences.

Occurrences like the one represented by Tobino are frequent due to the inadequacy or absence of interfaces. During the first months of 2020, Covid-19 confined a multitude of people within the home. Lockdown was the social innovation that forced them to review their relational behaviours. Between the enactment and extension of confinement measures and individual, social, and economic consequences, the devices to first mitigate and then provide alternatives to the negative spillovers were absent or ineffectual. Personal stress, tensions in the family and community environment, loss of spontaneous socialization, shutdowns, company closures and the fall of employment have burst into daily life.

NARRATIVE ECONOMICS

Economic language influences our interaction with nature. States of mind highlighted by works of fiction hide behind economic jargon. Stories offer a vivid illustration of events that change behaviour towards fellow human beings and nature.

Economic language changes according to the personal state of well-having and well-being, relationships and socioeconomic conditions prevailing in one's community. Fictional works portray different states of mind emerging from social contradictions invested by events capable of morphing human behaviour towards fellow human beings and nature.

During the Great Depression of the 1930s, the discourse revolved around the theme "more government versus more market." By forcing a renewal of economic thought and policy, the trauma caused by Covid-19 induced a review of contemporary narrative. It is instructive to (re)read *The Grapes of Wrath* (1939) by the American writer and Nobel Prize laureate in literature John Steinbeck (1902-1968). The passages reported here mirror the mood of hundreds of thousands of Midwestern families forced to abandon their farms. They were driven away by new technology (the tractor), climate change (dust storms), and financial greed (corporations owning banks that expropriated the farmers). The reading leads us to ponder civil society, the forgotten subject of the couple formed by the "government's public hand" and the market's "invisible hand." Steinbeck writes:

> *A half-million people moving over the country; a million more, restive to move; ten million more feeling the first nervousness. And tractors turning the multiple furrows in the vacant land.... Is a tractor bad? Is the power that turns the long furrows wrong? If this tractor were ours it would be good—not mine, but ours. If our tractor turned the long furrows of our land, it would be good. Not my land, but ours.... This is the beginning—from "I" to "we".... But that you cannot know. For the quality of owning freezes you forever into "I," and cuts you off forever form the "we."*

Far better than manifestos of intellectuals and white papers drawn up by expert commissions, Steinbeck's vivid portrait of the Great Depression shows in grand new language the collective "we" which is civil society. It is an open, non-corporate institution, made possible by the presence of citizens willing to cooperate with ethical values and a civic mentality that means reciprocity, altruism, and group identity within a framework of social norms. Such civic-minded citizenry has made the South Korean government's policies effective in combating Covid-19.

Homo oeconomicus, as an amoral individualist, took the lead in the 1980s with Margaret Thatcher (1925-2013) and Ronald Reagan (1911-2004), who headed the government in the United Kingdom and the United States, respectively. The "Iron Lady" claimed that there is no such thing as society. On the contrary, living in a symbiotic environment, the citizens of open civil society can produce concrete benefits for the benefit of all. They are economic and social actors together whose cooperative actions relieve public concern about increasing human, social, and economic costs from recurring epidemics, deterioration of the human habitat, and other extreme events.

The actors of change are caught up in the emotional turmoil of the knowledge economy, diverging from precepts that have defined it during past industrial revolutions. They revolted against *homo oeconomicus,* who wrote norms and dictated rules to exploit nature. Theirs is an act of creativity to explore nature's vast landscape, of which we know a very tiny part. The new economy springs from a foundation of creative ignorance which, emulating David Hume, formulates a "new science of man" based on the "experimental method." The abstract way of reasoning of *homo oeconomicus* is too narrow, focusing on morsels of nature. Around each of them, he raises high walls to protect himself from the environmental responsibility he bears. The new economy brings back to life the figure of the Renaissance man who, while experimenting, ignites the imagination, capable of breaking down walls to build bridges between human endeavours and the works of nature, between human-made and natural resources. Value outweighs money; quality matters over quantity. The athlete who in the old gymnasium of economics made his muscles with the anabolic drugs of reason will not listen to the voice of nature. It is the creative Renaissance experimenter who will listen.

Ideas are in and around us. We have to grab and use them to construct an engaging story that starts with "once upon a time." Great ideas travel on the wagon of chance. Seated on the wagon, supported by wheels of casual occurrence and unpredictability, the idea of coffee began its journey through time and space. Once upon a time, there was a young Yemenite shepherd named Kaldi who fed his flock with coffee berries. "Those fruit must be the work of the Devil," he pondered, noticing how the animals became agitated after eating them; and it was known that monks at the nearby Cheodet monastery regarded the berries as devilish and put them on their fires. The roasting process of the Cheodet monks caused the aroma of coffee to fill the air.

Scientists then arrived and started to reveal the book of nature and understand its secrets. Reading that book, Avicenna (980-1037), a Persian scientist and doctor of the eleventh century, promoted the therapeutic qualities of coffee, including it as a remedy in his *Canone di Medicina* (1025). Many other doctors were to follow his example and prescribe coffee as medicine, especially at the end of the seventeenth century. Thus, began a chain reaction that here we describe, in broad strokes, taking up the narrative unfolded in *The Red Thread of Coffee* (Formica, 2013).

The first "coffee shop" opened in Venice in 1683. Three years later, the first "literary café" in Paris—*Le Procope*—was opened by a Sicilian nobleman, Procopio dei Coltelli. With customers such as Voltaire, Diderot, and Fontanelle, *Le Procope* became the cradle of literary, philosophical, scientific, political, and artistic events. Since then, Italian artisans have kept alight the flame of tradition. In 1971, in Seattle, three intellectuals started a latter-day fire of innovation. Jerry Baldwin (a professor of English), Zev Siegel (a historian) and Gordon Bowker (a writer) opened their "Starbucks Coffee, Tea and Spice" stall in the city's main market square. The name Starbucks derives from Starbuck, the First Officer under Captain Ahab of the whaling ship Pequod, in Herman Melville's (1819-1891) novel *Moby Dick* (1851). So, Starbucks is a coffee house where imagination rides on waves of romanticism, roams and hunts in deep waters on the routes of the pioneers of the coffee trade between East and West. Starbucks started becoming a global brand when the creativity of Baldwin, Siegel, and Bowker came into contact with the commercial acumen of Howard Schultz. Complementing the intellectual skills of the three founders, Schulz contributed to innovation and change in coffeehouses worldwide, resulting in the now instantly recognizable, international brand.

In reading stories of successful craft and entrepreneurial vocations, one is often led to overlook their consequences on nature. The health benefits of coffee, the economic advantages for companies, and the job opportunities that stem from it are offset by damage caused by the discharge into rivers of waste produced by coffee processing plants. Contamination of water, vegetable, and animal environments harm the quality and growth of coffee beans. Reading stories like this one should then be enriched by the thinking whose source is the Roman poet Publius Ovidius Naso, known as Ovid (20 March 43 BC - 17/18 AD): "We dig the earth for solid gold not food" (Ovid, 2001). Be careful to consider coffee beans as if they were gold to be extracted from nature's quarries. Extractive capitalism can cause irreparable damage.

CAGE OF INEQUALITIES

Designers and storytellers face growing inequalities that threaten the health of the human hive and cause severe damage to the natural environment.

Vigorously shaken by the Covid-19 pandemic, will the human hive resist dissolution? Where and when will the human swarm settle materially and culturally? Will we experience the metamorphosis of the economic system? Much will depend on the course of inequalities, which have built a gilded cage for a few, a prison for many. Scholars of inequality in the distribution of income and wealth have raised the alarm. The Gini co-efficient, named after the statistician Corrado Gini (1884-1965) who conceived it, appears very sensitive to the trend of economic growth. The strongly unbalanced distribution of economic means worsens in the wake of a slow recovery and remains almost unchanged when the economy's pace accelerates.

In the game of forecasting that tries to glimpse light in the thick clouds enveloping the future, psychology is among the players. Interviewed by *The New York Times* in May 2020 (Bokat-Lindell, 2020), Paul Krugman remarked how the pandemic represents a different scenario than the 2008 crisis featuring the speculative bubble in the real estate sector and excessive debt. According to Krugman, winner of the 2008 Nobel Memorial Prize in Economic Sciences, we must consider the cognitive, emotional, and social processes affecting the economy. In the absence of an immunological response to Covid-19, people would learn to live with the new virus, as they have done with other mass death threats, and the economy would start running again faster than it did after 2008.

The deliberate construction of one's future stands in contrast to the game of forecasting. An original map, drawn along the way in *terra incognita*, replaces the intention of taking a path by consulting past trends. Exploration is more than justified by exceptional occurrences that shake the foundations on which community life rests. It is enough to reflect on these five adverse outcomes:

1. Boosted by Covid-19, the mode of work done from home benefits the most educated and relatively well-paid people, technology-intensive areas, and the wealthiest countries. The figures released by Jonathan Dingel and Brent Neiman (2020) are alarming. The two economists point out that "37 per cent of jobs in the United States can be performed entirely at home, with significant variation across cities and industries. These jobs typically pay more than jobs that cannot be done at home and account for 46 percent of all US wages. Applying our occupational classification to 85 other countries reveals that lower-income economies have a lower share of jobs that can be done at home."

2. A quarter to a third of jobs are thus vulnerable.

3. There has been a four-fold drop in employment of workers at the lower end of the wage scale compared to those at the top.

4. We have witnessed a persistent loss of employment among those with a low level of education.

5. Imbalances due to social distancing are exacerbated both by the accelerating pace of automation and by restrictions on the free movement of goods, services, capital, labour, technology, data, and information. Automated spaces, and others no longer viable for businesses due to mounting protectionist measures, have reduced the range of job opportunities; pharmaceutical, medical equipment, and food sectors are the most affected sectors.

Reprising the metaphor of the hive, let's consider an economic system as a living organism constituted of a crowd behaving as a unitary whole. Such a large group of people practises social solidarity as an antidote to disintegration. The emergence of such a social order requires will power. It is a self-struggle, fought with "feints, ruses, and strategic devices," to borrow the words of the economist Albert Hirschman (1915-2012; 1983), a fight against the usual way of life in pursuing the same desires through daily actions. Community involvement is a higher-order need that questions one's own identity, a "metapreference" that transcends the confines of the self. Unfolding events will tell whether the novel pandemic was the spark igniting the imagination for such a pervasive metamorphosis.

COMMON GOOD

Throughout the 2020 pandemic, the common good felt compelled to express itself, and it was able to do so. The human hive must show, and practice, empathy and desire for the public good.

The selfish, hostage of their attitude, have their feet firmly on the ground. The common good can move freely through the air. Alas, the common good often appears like *Little Thumb*, a child described by Charles Perrault (1628-1703) in the "Moral" of his fairy tales: "….sickly or slow-witted / He will be scorned, ridiculed, and despised / However, it is often the little urchin Who brings good fortune to the entire family" (Lang, 1889). "As a biologist," Jean Rostand says, "I know that man is a sociable animal. That he demands exchange, participation and affectivity. They are instincts and feelings to grow, remedies against alienation, antidotes against the anguish of our time" (Ronfani, 1972). And yet, in vacillating tournaments of the economy, man wears the armour of selfishness.

What moves the mind and ignites the passion, enacting behaviours that may lean either more towards personal and material preferences or more towards collective interests, even towards the whole of humanity? Setting the "tune" (a word derived from the late Latin *incentivum*) are the institutions that compose "melodies" (interventions) whose "phrases" (incentives) are predisposed to arouse "harmony" (reconciliation, correspondence) between individual interest and common good. These institutions, and among them the market that has gained a prominent role, are, however, imperfect instruments, subject to the turbulent values they uphold.

Disorder, inequality, and antagonism inherent in the market do not allow the natural order that is the economic equilibrium for the good of all, according to the vision of the economist and physician François Quesnay (1694-1774), founder of the Physiocratic school, and the economist and statesman Jacques Turgot (1727-1781). The intervention of political institutions, as maintained by Jacques Necker (1732-1804), Louis XVI's Minister of Finance, can remedy this, but to a limited extent. That engagement is also subject to loud disturbances, often triggered by pressure groups that pursue partisan politics to the detriment of community interests. Not only vested interests but also ideas can harm the public good, as Keynes feared (Strackey, 1956). Efficiency coupled with conspicuous consumption and waste, associated with conditions of relative deprivation, is one of those dangerous ideas.

Bellum omnium contra omnes, the war of all against all depicted by Thomas Hobbes (1588-1679), theorist of the social contract and state of nature, is the climate of mass society, with the market driving oversized accumulation of things. On the one hand is the egoists' desire for glory, an insatiable lust from which competition emerges with a warlike sign: "I win, you lose." On the other, we see the commodification of people in an atomized society made fragile by growing inequalities. Consequently, collective action is hard to achieve, if only for conflicts about the resources in which to invest. Such conflict is ignited by the fact that the energy expressed by society as a whole is less than the sum of its parts.

It is the vigorous shaking of the social and economic ground that projects a beam of light onto the public good. During the 2020 pandemic, the common good felt the need to express itself and was able to do so. Not to fall suddenly as unexpectedly as its word rose, people must show desire for the public good; we must express passion (which in Latin connotes the ability to suffer) for moving forward by embracing change. This feeling withers when the collective spirit is weak.

In which direction will the stream of opinion go? Will the mantle of order and stability continue to eclipse rising tides of inequality? Or will it celebrate a leaden egalitarianism disguised behind the words "progress" and "reform"? To reconcile competitive needs and social cohesion, selfish impulses and altruistic drives, John Stuart Mill's *On Liberty* (1859) is precious food for thought:

> *Unless opinions favourable...to property and to equality, to co-operation and to competition, to luxury and to abstinence, to sociality and individuality, to liberty and discipline, and all the other standing antagonisms of practical life, are expressed with equal freedom, and enforced and defended with equal talent and energy, there is no chance of both elements obtaining their due; one scale is sure to go up, and the other down.*

Especailly when a disease or other destructive event of extraordinary proportions jeopardizes the human assembly, "to prevent harm to others" is the indispensable Millian message that public authorities are called upon to triage.

HOMO EMPATHICUS

The common good takes care of man and nature. The treatment is empathy whose bearer is homo empathicus, who foretells the birth of communities that "feel inside" their members, "put themselves in their shoes," and do the same with nature.

When humanity is attacked by a crisis which prohibits a return to the habits and behaviours of the past, its accumulated capital trembles at the danger of crumbling into ruin. One human value, however, namely social capital, may counter that imminent risk. Social capital, consisting of trust, respect, and the creation of harmonious relationships, will continue to grow, even in situations of profound socioeconomic trauma, provided that the empathy factor comes into play. Volunteer corps, charitable organisations, civil service and various social networks assist people not to revert to the *status quo ante* but to guide them towards an unknown world. If physical proximity in time and space recoils due to the triggering event, empathy combined with digital technology yields proximity and social cohesion. The gauntlet thrown at society's feet by Covid-19 has opened doors to new and stronger social networks, thanks to empathy coupled with digital technology.

Disagreements that blossom into hostility and the elimination of doubt are cumulonimbus clouds that announce a social storm. What sweeps them away is the ability to understand and share the feelings, sensations, and emotions of others. The trust that comes from empathy forms cirrus clouds that indicate the appearance of pleasant social interactions. At the time of the Persian philosopher

Al-Ghazali (1058-1111), merchants with their trades were deemed bearers of trust and happiness. With the advent of the industrial revolution, the figure of the human being who obsessively pursues the goal of accumulating personal wealth, detached from thoughts for humanity, stood out with arrogance. In *A Christmas Carol*, Charles Dickens (1812-1870; 1843) vibrantly portrays the misanthrope, greedy and stingy Scrooge, the protagonist who turns empathic by rethinking his lifestyle:

> *The door to Scrooge's counting-house was open that he might keep an eye upon his clerk. [To warm himself] Scrooge had a very small fire, but the clerk's fire was so very much smaller that it looked like one coal.*

The boss plans to fire the employee if he ever tries to access the bucket of coal with the shovel in his hand. It was the speech of Marley's Ghost, his deceased partner that drove him to conversion.

> *Business!—cried the Ghost, wringing his hands again. Mankind was my business. The common welfare was my business; charity, mercy, forbearance, and benevolence, were, all, my business. The dealings of my trade were but a drop of water in the comprehensive ocean of my business.*

The selfish Scrooge archetype evokes *The Wealth of Nations* by Adam Smith (1776), an unintentional byproduct, or negative externality, of the idea that everyone would benefit from entrepreneurs driven to increase earnings and profits for their own personal interest. Such an objective would have meant more employment, more and new products and services, a higher entrepreneurial birth rate, and additional resources for scientific research. Why has this entrepreneurial intelligence not started a generative process of wealth and prosperity so widespread to grant economic dignity to all? On the contrary, in the unravelling of successive industrial revolutions, humanity has had to face waves of worsening inequality and the widening of precarious social strata (Azmanova, 2020). A consequence of excessive selfishness, or unenlightened self-interest ("I win, you lose") has been a deficit in the ability to perceive the world beyond one's *hortus conclusus*, the enclosed garden laden with exquisite and exclusive fruits (personal interests). In other words, the entrepreneurial intelligence that was objectively intended to solve problems and provoke opportunities has lacked the subjective consciousness that, as Smith wrote in *The Theory of Moral Sentiments* (1759), makes us interest ourselves in the well-being of others:

> *How selfish soever man may be supposed, there are evidently some principles in his nature, which interest him in the fortune of others, and render their happiness necessary to him, though he derives nothing from it except the pleasure of seeing it (Smith, 1853: 3).*

The idea of altruistic egoism ("I'm helping other people win so I can win, too") has not been taking root. To break down the high wall that secludes the garden from the outside world is *homo empathicus*, the producer of ideas that can prevail over forces aimed at preserving the past. Practising empathy gives rise to a climate of cooperation that allows everyone to tap into the portfolio of original ideas. The more discoveries are originated in public institutions, the more open will be the communities that spawned them. In the production of new things as a result of inventions, a multitude of companies would overtake monopolies and oligopolies (Stiglitz, 2020). Unique events such as those we are experiencing with increasing intensity and severe disruptions cannot be erased by limited and delayed access—real barriers raised by prohibitive prices—to innovative remedies that save lives and nature.

As understanding of studies in the fields of evolutionary biology, neuro-cognitive science, and child development—discoveries that reveal humanity's biological predisposition to empathy—grows, *homo empathicus* approaches centre stage of the human species, heralding the birth of communities founded on mutual understanding and active sympathy with nature. They are primarily physical communities where the words voiced can also be conveyed digitally. However, it is still in face-to-face dialogue that emotions are more easily and deeply understood. Physical gatherings facilitate instant exchange. The climate and terrain of exchanged words and objects produce the warm intimacy of relationships.

Empathy reflects the Smithian concept of sympathy assimilated to solidarity "with any emotion, not just with suffering or sorrow" (Rasmussen, 2020). Given the extreme interdependence between individual members, communities survive only as collective entities. They resemble the superorganism that is a colony of bees. Their high empathic quality prevailing over self-love distances them from the hive imagined by Bernard Mandeville, where luxury and injustice are as indispensable vices as hunger is necessary to drive us to eat (Mandeville, 1714). In empathic communities, the wealth leading to luxury and the power acting with the weapon of injustice are unusable keys to open the door of happiness. By tilling a happy mind and cultivating gardens of empathy for the public weal—not falling for uncritical Panglossian optimism—we pursue the ever-changing quest to repair our relationship with nature.

FRANKENSTEIN, OR HUMAN NATURE

Homo empathicus draws from Dr. Frankenstein's story the lesson that ideation is the way to recognize the interpenetration between the econosphere and the biosphere.

Acting in the econosphere, the sphere of the economy, yet neglecting the results of human actions on the biosphere: this is the spirit of yesterday's society that still lives in us today. Once upon a time, when from Galvinism the concept of electricity began to gain popularity, the scientist Victor Frankenstein, out of Mary Shelley's (1797-1851; 1818) pen, exploiting the power of electricity, artificially births a monster. The experiment of fabricating human life in a laboratory does not prevail. Before letting himself die, the nameless monster makes an accusation: "Am I to be thought the only criminal, when all human kind sinned against me?" Today, who are the monsters whose wrong and ugly creations damage the biosphere? The viral monster that surfaced in 2020 has received the name Covid-19, but many hypotheses remain hanging in the air about the anonymous creator. Did nature do it all on its own, or...? There are a range of inquiries, from scientific investigations to politically and economically motivated speculations. The latter also has the image of the monster that, living with its double, multiplies adverse effects.

Shelley's narrative, a forerunner of science fiction, raises the curtain on a scenario that encourages mental exuberance, an escape from thought conceived by the "Erewhonian method."

This is how Samuel Butler (1835-1902; 1872), the Victorian iconoclast author of the satirical work *Erewhon*, considered the Erewhonian "brains as a sort of sanctuary, to which if an opinion had once resorted, none other was to attack it." One flees the temple relying on the science that Butler defines as hypothetical because it prepares to face exceptional situations by probing the possibility of the existence of elusive natural elements.

By employing the materials, energy sources, and information available in the econosphere, we produce objects that interact with the biosphere both upstream during production and distribution processes and downstream once the discarded objects flow into nature reserves such as the atmosphere and the seas. We are therefore in the presence of a unique ecosystem whose "eco" and "bio" parts are never at rest, perpetually interacting and evolving.

There are those who would like the econosphere to be a reassuring world, in perpetual equilibrium, always still, inert, inanimate. That is a world that belongs to stories; for example, the world of Effi Briest, the protagonist of Theodor Fontane's (1818-1898; 1914) eponymous novel. Economic agents use physical technologies to manufacture things and provide services. In doing so, they resort to technologies, from blogs and social networks to web conferencing, to arrange people's work. The making is a cause of the disorder. To prepare an omelette, the cook breaks the eggs and then tidies up the kitchen. As the mathematician and economist Georgescu-Roegen (1906-1994) pointed out, the byproduct of spending energy to keep fighting economic entropy, disorder, is pollution.

There is no perfect quiet in the ecosystem. It was ultimately an illusion, the assumption of an achievable, perfect, and perpetual equilibrium through economic plans, in the manner of the Soviet Union. Their results were grounded on rational predictions drawn from accumulated knowledge and human behaviour presumed to be set once and for all. To prevent actions in the economic field exceeding the limit beyond which the ecosystem collapses, then uncertainty of the future, ignorance of what we do not know, ambiguity of interpretations of information, traps and cognitive prejudices scattered along the way—these all recommend avoiding the search for optimal solutions. Through humble investigations "satisfactory solutions," as Herbert Simon calls them, become discernible for an environmentally sustainable economy.

From Dr. Frankenstein, the monster's creator, we learn that the will to cross the threshold of the known leads to two forked paths. One is dark, crossed by hostile forces inherent in development, be it scientific, social or economic. The other is enlightened, paved with the ideation that makes the world more understandable and friendly. Those aware of the inextricable link between the econosphere and the biosphere can travel the second path.

ROUTES OF SCIENCE

Science and industry are leading players in the natural and the human world. Some scientists explore the two worlds by ploughing the vast ocean of nescience with knowledge maps on which they chart their course. Experimenting with ignorance as a source of creativity, others glimpse new routes. There are also scientists seeking business opportunities that only long hence will appear evident to everyone. For them, tackling the unreasonable is not a risk but a sport that is worth practising to achieve the impossible.

Science is in constant motion, powered by imagination. New ways of understanding supplant previous views. As 2020 dawned, scientists began to plough the perilous sea of Covid-19. They are committed to providing answers to difficult questions. On the knowledge map, navigator-explorers plotted their course. Having passed the Pillars of Hercules, the vast ocean of non-knowledge opens to their eyes. Moving with their minds within the boundaries of knowledge, they observe what everyone can see, but they come to think and plan what was never before considered. Without maps, other navigators rely on the current of ignorance to capture what the well-informed explorers cannot perceive. Thus, tension stirs between, on the one hand, deductions of path finders who navigate pre-mapped routes and, on the other hand, intuitions of path creators who glimpse new routes via creative ignorance. Occupying the space of not knowing, these creative ignoramuses undertake an adventure that carries them from John Milton (1608-1674) to follow in the footsteps of William

Shakespeare (1564-1616), as interpreted by William Hazlitt (1778-1830; 1821). In the words of the English essayist and literary critic, those creatives exhibit

> *most exuberance of invention and the greatest freedom from prejudice. Shakespeare's was evidently an uneducated mind, both in the freshness of his imagination and the variety of his views; as Milton's was scholastic, in the texture both of his thoughts and feelings....If we wish to know the force of human genius we should read Shakespeare.*

A third route directs scientists to industrial laboratories. The academic building is not the only one hosting science. In an interview following the publication of his book *The Scientific Life*, Steven Shapin (2008), historian and sociologist of science at Harvard University, noted that:

> *If we look at the pure research done in industry and that done in academia, many of the most popular contrasts describe the situation rather poorly. If autonomy is the issue, many industrial scientists from early in the twentieth century enjoyed as much of that as their academic colleagues. And the same applies to notions of secrecy and openness. A clear contrast of quality between university and industrial science similarly seems not to hold, while a presumption that applied research and development requires less brain-power than pure research is just dogmatic.*

Those rummaging through the drawers of science proceed along two other routes: publication in the most prestigious international journals and the entrepreneurial translation of scientific discovery. The Renaissance put art and science at the centre of value creation. In the Age of Reason, under the spotlights of Enlightenment and Rationality, an informal learning club was founded in Birmingham: The Lunar Society, so-called because the meetings, held regularly between 1765 and 1813, took place at every full moon, at dinner time. It was a diverse body of visionaries, including scientists, inventors, entrepreneurs, artisans, artists, and politicians who shared ideas freely, unfettered by interference or influence arising from monetary incentives. Among the Lunaticks, there were personalities the likes of the chemist Joseph Priestley (1733-1804), the inventor James Watt (1736-1819), the entrepreneur Josiah Wedgwood (1730-1795), the manufacturer and Watt's business partner Matthew Boulton (1728-1809), and the physician, naturalist, and poet Erasmus Darwin (1731-1802). By making science, art, and commerce interact, those brilliant minds intertwined new technologies of the industrial revolution with the commerce of the liberal revolution.

In our times, the production of knowledge revolves towards entrepreneurial action with scientists wearing entrepreneurial clothes creatively designed by experiences gained along scientific paths. A representative figure of knowledge in action is the entrepreneurial scientist who weaves the threads of knowledge with those of doing. Entrepreneurial scientists can help transform the most complex problems of research into enterprises. Scientific discoveries, innovations, and entrepreneurship produce increasing returns. So many nudges come into action to move the enormous boulders of conservatism.

The interplay between science and entrepreneurship accelerates the impact of discoveries on human behaviour. In the Victorian age, writes Clive Thompson (2019), scientists, beginning with Eunice Newton Foote (1819-1888), an amateur scientist and distinguished suffragette, conducted the first experiments proving that out-of-control carbon dioxide could one day cook the planet. If a business process had been set in motion quickly, in line with the scientific investigations, then understanding of climate change would have been faster and more widespread, and the remedies against global warming would have been accelerating.

EDUCATION EXPERIMENT

More than the digital gap must be bridged. There is also the macabre dance of the cognitive divide in which skeletons personify today's schools, and learners represent the agents of the future. They do not want to end up buried beneath the debris of education's crumbling edifice.

Covid-19 has jeopardised learning; kicked him out of classrooms. To prevent learning from being taken away from the new generations, educational authorities have intervened on the organisational front of the school sector, first and foremost with distance learning through new technologies. Pupils in poorer countries and communities suffer from a lack of access to adequate broadband services. They and their peers in countries with better economic conditions are facing fewer opportunities as their inadequate curricula are poorly designed to cope with waves of technological, productive, and social change.

To prevent the worst, schools have to drop the old fiction. It is not enough to add to the legacy left by predecessors. Schools must create a new narrative. The nature of education is called to make an abrupt change, embracing three exhortations (one should, one could, one will) that evoke four knowledges (knowing how to do, think, imagine, understand) submitted to experimentation. Attempts and trials arise from this question: having automated the muscles during the industrial revolution, are we automating the brain during the current cognitive revolution, with potentially enormous economic and social repercussions?

Experimentation involves not only the expert, the peritus from which the verb *experiri* derives, but also the creative ignoramus whose sense of possibility urges action to realize the potential of plausible events. Through experimentation and experience, we can re-imagine education, as highlighted in a previous work (Formica, 2020), which configures the learning revolution. These are its distinctive features:

1. Nurturing the imagination and cultivating the open-mindedness of pupils, who can then direct their passions and pursue original ideas—an epiphany of original thoughts that challenge the *status quo*.

2. Letting students practice the intellectual gymnasium in which the different branches of knowledge interact until they merge. By building transdisciplinary bridges, students will be able to design their tailor-made study clothes, merging scientific and humanistic subjects. Among the "tools" of the gym, narratives shed light on possible pathways. Think of the human story of the German Jesuit Athanasius Kircher (1602-1680), a scientific star of the Baroque age and a traveller in many worlds of knowledge. Kircher moved between the study of volcanoes and fossils, the observation of microbes under the microscope, mechanical inventions such as automata, the magnetic clock and megaphone, Egyptology, music theory, and comparative religion.

3. Allowing pupils to swim in the waters of doubt, where conventional thinking is in danger. Not to drown, the swimmers' minds must be free to move, not exposed to the scrutiny of experts looking for possible heresies. Nor, even worse, should they be subject to the control of sponsors who judge as heresy those ideas that are at odds with their own judgments and opinions. It was the American economist John Kenneth Galbraith who denounced the extent to which commercial companies financing colleges and universities were keeping in check academic opinions counter to their perceived needs.

4. Aiming at the richness of diversity and the intensity of interactions for learning. In this respect, John Stuart Mill's *On Liberty* (1859) is illustrative:

   > *It is individuality that we war against: we should think we'd done wonders if we'd made ourselves all alike; forgetting that the unlikeness of one person to another is generally the first thing which draws the attention of either to the imperfection of his own type, and the superiority of another, or the possibility, by combining the advantages of both, of producing something better than either...Mankind speedily became unable to conceive diversity, when they have been for some time unaccustomed to see it.*

HOW STARRY IS THE MANUFACTURING SKY?

Industrial manufacturing has continued to see stars even in the gray smog of fossil-fuel-hungry factories. Environmental responsibility has been neglected. Once the culture of entrepreneurship that cares for the socioeconomic environment while respecting nature appears on the horizon, the time machine to revive Renaissance workshops, in the 3D version, comes into action. Laboratories of intellectual blossoming, such workshops celebrate the figure of the ideator who combines science and entrepreneurship, and both with nature.

As the industrial revolution unfolded, the manufacturing landscape changed. Its prevailing geographical aspect is no longer the set of non-agricultural production activities carried out by a multitude of manufacturers in a given location. Manufacturing concentrates in the factory populated by a mass of workers and machines. Above it the sky appeared starry, each star pointing to a job created, to a new machine in operation. In short, more employment and more investment; but that is not all. In the Smithian vision illustrated in *The Wealth of Nations* (1776), together with trade, manufacturing produces good governance, order, security, and personal liberty from which the lower classes benefit. Economic development has accelerated quicker than in the past. Gray of smog from fossil-fuel-hungry factories was willfully ignored. Large manufacturing plants have continued to see stars. Environmental responsibility has been neglected.

While industrial manufacturing has enjoyed the panorama of a star-studded sky, has it grown within itself the moral law that gives workers personality to make themselves autonomous, to be independent from the regulatory mechanisms of the factory system? The execution of parcelled tasks subject to managerial command and control, compounded by the practice of "divide and rule" to ban the formation of coalitions among the wage earners and make them rivals of each other: this is the invisible chain that has bound the workers' personalities and prevented the manifestation of their character. The strength of arms and legs has been rewarded over the might of free and extroverted thought.

Covid-19 has deposed the factory's supremacy as a workplace *par excellence*. Even before the epidemic broke out, with the development of digital technologies, there were already early signs of returning home to carry out one's tasks in teleworking and "smart working" mode. Social distancing accelerated the trend. The current phenomenon is a great social experiment bearing a swarm of virtues that, however, could turn into vices. By surfing the Internet Ocean, the worker can reach many places. Working from home, the employee potentially enriches personal well-being (less stress, better work-life balance) and the environment (less pollution). In order not to turn virtue into vice, the teleworker must not become isolated.

"I miss the social interaction of the office" is a strong call from the workers. Only experimentation will tell how effective virtual, digitally well-qualified work teams that draw on their members' knowledge can be. More than speed and productivity are at stake. Innovation is also on the line. Thriving in the emergent world requires discovering routes to innovate. "Smart working" helps trace the path to the New World. What makes the difference is not working from home, but doing so in collaboration with tribes different from ours. There is no need for specialized technologies beyond a smartphone, a laptop, or a tablet. Instead, it is essential that companies reward the creativity of employees and organizes work according to objectives and results. The same goes for the passion and the ability of the employee to propose herself as a creator who promotes and participates in casual meetings and free conversations, not only thanks to the internet but also by crossing the virtual with the real (face to face).

The world before us compels new combinations of knowledge and ideas. The economy train must equip itself to run wagons where so many workers and so many machines are no longer crowded. The quantity of GDP growth must no longer neglect the quality of progress. The best use of smart working is to cultivate a generation of ideators who, like the three princes of Serendip (the ancient name of the island of Sri Lanka), make discoveries, by chance and sagacity, of things they were not seeking. Serendipity also requires a certain restlessness, the desire to keep moving, because one cannot stumble into the unexpected by standing still.

Experimentation induces one to think of ways of acting that are foreign to subordinate work. Muhammad Yunus, Nobel Peace Prize winner and social entrepreneur, claims that human beings are born entrepreneurs, not job seekers. This message from the founder of Grameen Bank and pioneer of micro-credit has made us glimpse in the darkness of Covid-19 the dawn of a new age whose culture of entrepreneurialism will care for the socioeconomic environment while respecting nature.

Resuming what we argued in *Econaissance: The Reimagined School and the Culture of Entrepreneurialism* (Formica, 2020), if the image of entrepreneurialism is blurred, it means that it is struggling to assert itself as an art that, by grasping ideas to open the doors of the future, converts them into an entity called "Transformative

Enterprise." Entrepreneurialism flourishes when nonconformist experimenters meet and interact in informal groups. They are amateurs and pragmatists, not just academics. On the other hand, the minor recurrence of the word "entrepreneurship" suggests that the managerial economy has gradually overwhelmed the entrepreneurial economy. Unlike the latter, the former is identified with business as synonymous with material prosperity. Entrepreneurialism and its translation into entrepreneurship are, above all, ways of perceiving the world that contribute to the broader design of society, feeding a social movement that challenges the business model that sees the creation of value for shareholders as a fixed point around which the company revolves.

For manufacturing, this time in the presence of the moral law is a new starry sky. The task is entrusted to entrepreneurs of social progress, achieved by inventing revolutionary ways of working, offering products and services, and seeing the world. The industrial revolution has created jobs. With the knowledge revolution, workers are replaced by ideators who train in the gymnasium of creative thinking. They transport thoughts from one mind to another. Great travellers on par with the philosopher and scientist René Descartes (1596-1650), the ideators open the "great book of the world" interacting with people of diverse temperaments and all walks of life. Mutual exchange produces new knowledge. The more knowledge is gained, the more one knows how much remains to discover. Progress reveals itself in the ideators' occupations which are no longer the inhuman toil of which Cesare Pavese (1906-1950; 1968) poetised. Their professions are activities of thought carried out in digital and hybrid form, merging the world of bytes and the world of atoms (Formica, 2020).

Many are the roads that lead to the land of entrepreneurship where extraordinary phenomena occur. If the trade routes carry diseases, in that land along the paths of knowledge, ideas and technologies are moving that design new ways of being. Covid-19 has accelerated the speed at which technology, coupled with revolutionary mental models, pushes to the margins the mass factory with its products for an undifferentiated multitude of consumers. The change is visible in companies that discard economies of scale to focus on customized offerings. "Doing it just in time" gives way to "making it right for that given single person." Efficacy is rewarded rather than being sacrificed on the altar of efficiency.

One does not curl up like a hedgehog to face the storm of change but relies on resilience—that is, the ability to adapt to a traumatic event by taking advantage of the opportunities it offers. Production is made in small batches and close to customers. Through the widespread diffusion of 3D machines, the factory is decentralised in many places, operated by people who are creators and entrepreneurs. That is the opposite of the current situation, which sees so many machines assembled in large factories where workers are called to execute orders coming from "thinking machines." No more a thousand machines in one place, but one machine in a thousand places, as the co-founder of 3D Hubs, Bram de Zwart (Maney, 2020) put it.

Is it already in action, the time machine to bring Renaissance workshops back to life and, with them, the ideal embodiment of the "cultural consumer" in the figure of Isabella d'Este (1474-1539), Marquise of Mantua? She did not resort to the intermediation of distributors, but she attended the marketplaces in person, near shops which offered tailor-made creations. The factory of mass production has guaranteed employment and income.

Employment means being occupied, absorbed by duties imposed by others at the top of hierarchical organisational structures with rigid long-range plans.

The 3D workshop is a laboratory of intellectual blossoming. Each person is an ideator engaged in the creation and experimentation of ideas to share and develop with others. This triggers fundamental innovation processes followed by plummeting product development costs, already reduced by a factor of 10 over the last decade. There is in embryo a high birth rate of entrepreneurial realities in life sciences, energy, and cleantech capable of benefiting the whole living world. Many independent manufacturers are now willing to share ideas and to finance and co-own new shops. As with manufacturing in the past, they have a marketplace outside their door: just taking short online walks around the world, surfing the internet and acting like sea turtles, which explore faraway places and then lay their eggs (ideas and projects) at home.

POWER OF IMAGINATION

We have sketched a drawing along the course of the Covid-19 event. Faced with holes of ignorance dug by the virus, we can fill them by finding new ways of thinking and acting. Narratives lead us to reflect by opening the window on future possibilities to be seen through the eyes of the imagination.

Imagination redesigns how we look at things. Then we discover new scenarios in which things, seen from other angles, change. It is no longer unimaginable to demarcate the economy into two kinds of added value: one that we get from exploiting nature's resources; the other growing from our relations with nature. In the first meaning, "man is the measure to all things," claiming to be too intelligent to be satisfied with what exists. New methods are always found for extracting resources, at the expense of nature. In the second sense, man is part of a whole.

Progress has risen to myth. It is the Victorian tale of an irreversible change in the direction of material improvement. This mythological statue has been shaken deeply by Covid-19 and will end up overturning if the axe of material progress that disrespects nature is not removed. The idea of progress whose roots are social and cultural is therefore under question. It has caused an unprecedented transformation of the biosphere. Recalling once again Ovid (2001), who describes a Golden Age when "...no one cut the earth with a sturdy plough, nor did the land surveyor delimit the land with any boundary," one must recall the history of how people interact with each other and the environment.

Through analysis of the specificities of history and culture, we will come to find a space for fruitful interactions with nature, leaving behind the present age, the Anthropocene. There are no laws that remain unchanged as situations change. The first to vary is the law of measurement, which narrows knowledge down to quantitative evaluations. Pretending that the measure of highest personal profit coincides with the profit of others, the law of self-interest has produced, for example, colonialism and slavery, forerunners of the Anthropocene. Both, besides human damage, have altered the ecological balance. "The impact of colonialism was so profound it can be detected in Earth's air and rocks," reports science journalist Robin McKie (2018). Data are useful, but not if disconnected from the historical and cultural context depicted in narratives, which flourish in the land of history and culture and are preferable to numbers when the physicality and hardness of measurements seems excessive.

On that land, the building of creative learning is to be erected. Here are born and circulate the transformative ideas whose productivity is not measured in quantitative terms, as the difference between input and output, but consists in the quality of the growth dividend attributed to the ecologically, and not only economically, sustainable businesses that arise from those ideas. Creative learning is like the canary in the coal mine that reveals the presence of elements harmful to nature. The canary of creative learning is not some omniscient ideologue who bases his judgment on the presumed precision of predictive models whose bricks are rational expectations. Conscious of living in a world of imperfect knowledge, the canary's thinking mind looks around, asks questions, listens to the voice of nature, and assesses what is happening in the mine of humanity. It pays attention to the quality of human activity both in the economy and in society, accepting uncertainty, being open to the unknown, trusting intuition to look ahead and freeing the mind to wander.

Covid-19 calls our evolutionary age to reach a higher peak of cognitive abilities. It is a cultural moment, a turning point, which places a daisy on the barrel of the gun pointed at nature. Adverse effects on nature exercised by industrial society are counterbalanced by the canary who from the coal mine raises the alarm as it flies towards the society of knowledge and ideation.

AFTERWORD

Brian Donnellan

Professor Piero Formica has provided a wise and insightful exploration of the ebb and flow of the uneasy relationship between Humankind and Nature down through the ages. He weaves a fine thread across seemingly disparate intellectual traditions to create a timely, unique perspective on one of the Grand Challenges of our time–Health, culminating in a thoughtful analysis of our current struggle to come to grips with the Covid-19 virus.

Prof. Formica, in this treatise, reminds us that there is much to be learned from the history and literature of our efforts to overcome health pandemics—if we choose to engage with that body of knowledge. He invokes Ronald Wright as someone who has engaged with the lessons of history. Wright (2004) reminds us that the unsavoury

> *truth is that until the middle ages, most cities were death traps, seething with disease, vermin, and parasites and that the average life expectancy in ancient Rome was only nineteen or twenty years and only slightly better than in Britain's Black Country, evoked so vividly by Dickens, where the average age fell to seventeen...*

One is reminded of Hegel's claim that "We learn from history that we do not learn from history." In the case of pandemics, there have been many salutary tales. In 1348 Boccaccio was 35 when he wrote about the Black Death pandemic. The text could well have been written today:

> *What made this pestilence all the more virulent was that it was spread by the slightest contact between the sick and the healthy just as a fire will catch dry or oily materials when they are placed right beside it. In fact this evil went further, for not only did it infect those who merely talked or spent any time with the sick, but it also appeared to transfer the disease to anyone who merely touched the clothes or other objects that had been handled or used by those who were its victims (Boccaccio, The Decameron, Day 1).*

In 1585 the mayor of Bordeaux during the bubonic plague, Michel de Montaigne, was self-isolated in his chateau and wrote his *Essais*. In his final essay, "On Experience," he reveals that "greatness of soul is not so much pressing upward and forward as knowing how to circumscribe and set oneself in order." Today, the Covid-19 lockdown is providing some people with the mental space to re-visit personal value systems and take stock of our place in the world. The term "mindfulness" had not been coined in the 1500s but Montaigne's call to use self-isolation as an opportunity to "set oneself in order" has clear resonances today.

In 1664, in the early pages of *A Journal of the Plague Year*, Daniel Defoe (1660-1731) reports that local authorities in some neighbourhoods of London tried to make the number of plague deaths appear lower than it was by registering other, invented diseases as the recorded cause of death. Today, in the era of "fake news" we witness controversy around apparent underreporting and mis-representing of facts surrounding the pandemic.

In 1827, Alessandro Manzoni (1785-1873) wrote his classic novel *The Betrothed*, in which he supports the Milanese citizens' anger at the official response to the 1630 plague. Manzoni showed that the plague spread rapidly because the restrictions introduced were insufficient, their enforcement was lax, and his fellow citizens did not heed them. The challenges of devising and enforcing "lockdown" are indeed still with us.

Another strong theme in Formica's work is our constant striving to achieve solidarity and collective responsibility in times of economic strife. Here there are resonances with contributions from Luce and Sennet. Luce holds that economic growth is the unifying force for liberal democracies, and when that growth stalls or falls, things tend to take a dark turn. The "left-behinds" seek scapegoats for their woes, and consensus becomes harder to reach as politics devolves increasingly into a zero-sum game. Sennet identifies healthcare as an acute example of the need to protect society's weakest from arbitrary misfortune; the ultimate test of our civilizational worth, universal healthcare ought to be a basic shield against the vicissitudes of an ever more volatile economic environment. In his view, the new forms of capitalism emphasize short-term labour and institutional fragmentation; the effect of this economic system has been that workers cannot sustain supportive social relations with one another. Hence ordinary people are driven back on themselves, as they crave some sort of solidarity of us-against-them.

Formica is sensitive to what he sees as our over-reliance on technology as a panacea for our current travails, a theme echoed in James Bridle's recent work which warns against a future in which the promise of a new technologically-assisted Enlightenment may just deliver its opposite: an age of complex uncertainty, predictive algorithms, surveillance, and the hollowing out of empathy. Bridle contends that the enormity of challenges such as pandemics are hard to grasp, and that real change could only be effected by a great mass of individuals acting cohesively. The critical issue is that technologies such as social media can atomise rather than fuse our social formations.

An overarching theme in Formica's distinguished career to date and that persists in this work is the need for an interdisciplinary approach to addressing Grand Challenges such as Health. He rails against single-minded, doctrinaire attempts to analyse such challenges and sees Art and Science not as marginal specialisms but rather as universal possessions of humanity, and vital contributory parts of our species' repertory. In this sense, Formica takes his place in the school of thinkers advocating unity in natural sciences, social sciences, and humanities—including such luminaries as Snow and Wilson.

Formica's thought processes and rationale have much in common with Wilson's view that liberal arts students should be helped to understand that in the twenty-first century the world will not be run by those who possess mere information alone. Both argue for more synthesis. Wilson's assertion that "We are drowning in information, while starving for wisdom. The world henceforth will be run by synthesizers, people able to put together the right information at the right time, think critically about it, and make important choices wisely" aligns well with Formica's worldview.

Finally, Formica makes a strong case for the power of narrative and the significance of what he calls *homo narrans*. Here we find a fundamentally optimistic note that resonates with Pinker's identification of the importance of narrative. As Pinker (2018) writes in *Enlightenment Now* (2018), human progress is

> *not just a matter of debunking fallacies or disseminating data. It may be cast as a stirring narrative, and I hope that people with more artistic flair and rhetorical power than I can tell it better and spread it farther. The story of human progress is truly heroic. It is glorious. It is uplifting. It is even, I daresay, spiritual...and the story belongs not to any tribe but to all of humanity, to any sentient creature with the power of reason and the urge to persist in its being. For it requires only the convictions that life is better than death, health is better than sickness, abundance is better than want, freedom is better than coercion, happiness is better than suffering, and knowledge is better than superstition and ignorance.*

Luce shares Formica's fundamental faith in our ability to tackle the Grand Challenges through reasoned debate and narrative: "The West's crisis is real, structural and likely to persist," he writes. "Nothing is inevitable. Some of what ails the West is within our power to fix." Doing so means rejecting complacency about democracy and our system's resilience, and "understanding exactly how we got here."We see in our daily news that the cadence of the global spread of Covid-19 is relentless and can be modelled scientifically as an exponential phenomenon. Meanwhile our artists and social commentators are scrambling to develop and portray a human response in the face of competing and conflicting societal forces. At the heart of Formica's latest work is a call to arms to achieve synchronicity in our collective response to Nature's challenges. Depicting the enormous complexity of this task can appear so daunting as to be beyond language—scientific or artistic. The great Polish poet Czesław Miłosz advises us to turn to poetry when prose fails us. In his poem "Preface" he counsels,

Novels and essays serve but will not last.
One clear stanza can take more weight
than a whole wagon of elaborate prose.

So perhaps, we should follow Formica's guidance to look beyond formulaic argumentation and domain-specific discourse to help us express the need for synchronicity between Humankind and Nature. The Irish poet Seamus Heaney put it well:

History says don't hope
On this side of the grave.
But then, once in a lifetime
The longed for tidal wave
Of justice can rise up
And hope and history rhyme.

REFERENCES

Abe, Naoko. *"Cherry" Ingram: The Englishman Who Saved Japan's Blossoms*. London: Chatto & Windus, 2019.

Ahmad, Talmiz. "Keeping Faith in Times of Pestilence Often Meant Inventing New Enemies," *The Wire*, April 11, 2020.

Atwater, Peter. "The gap between the haves and the have-nots is widening sharply," *Financial Times*, June 10, 2020.

Avicenna. *Canone di Medicina*, 1025.

Azmanova, Albena. "Precarity, not inequality is what ails the 99%," *Financial Times*, April 28, 2020.

Bauman, Zygmunt. *Vita liquida*, Bari: Laterza, 2006. Original edition: *Liquid life*, Cambridge, UK: Polity Press, 2005.

Berlin, Isaiah. *The Hedgehog and the Fox: An Essay on Tolstoy's View of History*, London: Weidenfeld & Nicolson, 1953.

Boccaccio, Giovanni. *The Decameron*. United Kingdom: Oxford University Press, 1998.

Bokat-Lindell, Spencer. "How Long Will It Take for the Economy to Recover?" *New York Times*, May 22, 2020.

Borges, Jorge Luis. "On exactitude in science," in A. Hurley (Trans.), *Collected fictions* (p. 325). New York: Viking Penguin, 1998. Original edition: "Del rigor en la ciencia," *Los Anales de Buenos Aires*, anno 1, no.3, 1946.

Bridle, James. *New Dark Age: Technology and the End of the Future.* New York: Verso, 2018.

Butler, Samuel. *Erewhon or Over the Range*. London: Trübner & Co., 1872.

Camus, Albert. *The Plague*. United States: Knopf Doubleday Publishing Group, 2012.

Crevel, Rene. *Paul Klee*. Paris: Gallimard, 1930.

Cronin, A. J. *The Citadel*. London: Gollancz; Boston: Litte, Brown, 1937.

Deaton, Angus. "Angus Deaton Says More: An interview," Project Syndicate, February 18, 2020.

Defoe, Daniel. *A Journal of the Plague Year*. Harmondsworth: Penguin, 1966. Original work published 1722.

Dickens, Charles. *A Christmas Carol*, London: Chapman & Hall, 1843.

Dingel, J. and Neiman, B. "How Many Jobs Can be Done at Home?" Becker Friedman Institute for Economics at the University of Chicago, June 19, 2020.

Eliot, T. S. *The Complete Poems and Plays*, 1909-1950. San Diego, California: Harcourt Brace & World, 1951.

Feyerabend, Paul. K. *Der Wissenschaftstheoritische Realismus un die Autorität der Wissenschaften*, Braunschweig: Vieweg & Sohn, 1978.

Fontane, Theodor. *Effi Briest*, New York: German Publication Society, 1914. *Effi Briest*, Stuttgart: Philipp Reclam jun., 1895.

Formica, Piero. *Stories of Innovation for the Millennial Generation: The Lynceus Long View*. New York: Palgrave Macmillan, 2013.

Formica, Piero. "The Innovative Coworking Spaces of 15th-Century Italy," *Harvard Business Review*, April 27, 2016. https://hbr.org/2016/04/the-innovative-coworking-spaces-of-15th-century-italy.

Formica, Piero. *The Role of Creative Ignorance: Portraits of Path Finders and Path Creators*: New York: Palgrave Macmillan, 2014.

Formica, Piero. *Econaissance: The School Reimagined and the Culture of Entrepreneurialism*, Bingley, UK: Emerald Publishing, 2020.

Franklin, Benjamin. *Mémoires de la vie privée de Benjamin Franklin*, Paris: Buisson, 1791.

Gaffney, Owen. "11 reasons bees matter," World Economic Forum, February 29, 2016.

Global Coffee Report, *New research shows impact of bees on coffee productivity*, May 29, 2018 (https://gcrmag.com/news/article/new-research-shows-impact-of-bees-on-coffee-productivity).

Goethe, Johann Wolfgang. *Teoria della natura* (English translations by Piero Formica). Milano: SE, 2020.

Greenberg, Aaron and AJ. *Recorded Time: How to Write the Future*, Chicago: bioGraph, 2020.

Hazlitt, William. *Table Talk: Essays on Men and Manners*, London, UK: Henry Frowde, 1821.

Heaney, Seamus. "Doubletake" in the "The Cure of Troy." New York: Farrar, Straus, and Giroux, 1990.

Heffernan, Margaret. "Treat workers like robots and they might behave like them," *Financial Times*, February 25, 2020.

Hirschman, Albert O. *Shifting Involvements. Private Interest and Public Action*, Princeton: Princeton University Press, 1982.

Kilpatrick, Donna. "A farming revolution is what we need in this crisis," *Financial Times*, July 31, 2020.

Klee, Paul. *Paul Klee: The Bauhaus Years Works from 1918-1932*, Ed. Olivier Berggruen, New York: Dickinson Roundell, 2013.

Lang, Andrew. *The Blue Fairy Book*, London: Longmans, Green, and Co., ca. 1889, pp. 231-241. Lang's source: Charles Perrault, *Histoires ou contes du temps passé, avec des moralités: Contes de ma mère l'Oye*. Paris, 1697.

Leopardi, Giacomo. *Zibaldone: The Notebooks of Leopardi*, Caesar, M. and D'Intino, F., eds, London, UK: Penguin Classics, 2013.

Luce, Edward. *The Retreat of Western Liberalism*, Little, Brown, 2017.

Mandeville, Bernard. *The Fable of the Bees: or, Private Vices, Publick Benefits*, London: J. Roberts, 1714.

Maney, Kevin. "How Covid-19 is reversing economies of scale," strategy + business, May 7, 2020.

Manzoni, Alessandro. *I promessi sposi*. Pisa, 1827; *The Betrothed Lovers*, translated by Charles Swan.

Melville, Herman. (1851). *Moby Dick*, London: Penguin, 2009.

Mill, John Stuart. *On Liberty*, London: John W. Parker and Son, 1859.

Milosz, Czeslaw. *A Treatise on Poetry*, New York: Ecco Press, 2001.

Montaigne, Michel de. *The Complete Essays*, London: Penguin Classics, 1993.

Nelson, Julie. "What Is Radical Economics? (Hint: It's Not Neoliberal or Marxist)," *Evonomics*, January 29, 2017

Nuland, Sherwin. *The Doctor's Plague. Germs, Children Fever, and the Strange Story of Ignác Semmelweis*, New York and London: W. W. Norton & Company, 2003.

O'Neill, Jim. "A v-shaped recovery could still happen," Project Syndicate, July 7, 2020.

Ovid. *The Love Poems*, Book III, a translation into English by A. S. Kline. PiT (Poetry In Translation – *www.poetryintranslation.com*), 2001.

Pamuk, Orhan. "What the Great Pandemic Novels Teach Us," *New York Times*, April 23, 2020.

Papini, Giovanni. *Il Tragico quotidiano*, Firenze: Lumachi, 1906.

Pavese, Cesare. *Hard Labor, in: The Selected Works of Cesare Pavese*, New York: Farrar, Straus and Giroux, 1968. *Lavorare stanca*. Firenze: Edizioni di Solaria, 1936.

Pinker, Steven. *Enlightenment Now*, London: Allen Lane, 2018.

Poincaré. Henri. *La Science et l'Hypothèse*, Paris: Flammarion, 1902.

Rasmusssen, Dennis. C. *The Infidel and the Professor. David Hume, Adam Smith, and the Friendship That Shaped Modern Thought*, Princeton: Princeton University Press, 2017.

Ronfani, Ugo. *Salotto parigino*. Milano: Pan editrice, 1972.

Roubini, Nouriel. "A Greater Depression?," Project Syndicate, March 24, 2020.

Roubini, Nouriel. "Revisiting the White Swans of 2020," Project Syndicate, July 29, 2020.

Satel, Greg. "The Limited Value of Ideas, Medium," *Medium*, September, 28, 2019.

Sciascia, Leonardo. *La scomparsa di Majorana*, Torino: Einaudi, 1975.

Sennett, Richard. *Together: The Rituals. Pleasures and Politics of Cooperation*. New York: Penguin, 2012.

Serres, Michel. *Hominescence*, Paris: Le Pommier, 2001.

Shapin Steven. *The Scientific Life: A Moral History of a Late Modern Vocation*. Chicago: University of Chicago Press, 2008.

Shelley, Mary. *Frankenstein; or, The Modern Prometheus*. London: Printed for Lackington, Hughes, Harding, Mavor, & Jones Publisher, 1818.

Shiller, Robert. J. "Narrative Economics," Cowles Foundation discussion paper no. 2069, January 2017.

Short, Robert L. *The Parable of Peanuts*, New York: United Feature Syndicate, 1968.

Smith, Adam. *The Theory of Moral Sentiments*. London: Henry G. Bohn, 1853. Original work published 1759.

Smith, Adam. *An Inquiry into the Nature and Causes of the Wealth of Nations*, London: W. Strahan and T. Cadell, 1776.

Snow, Charles. *The Two Cultures*. Cambridge University Press, 1959.

Spence, Michael and Chen Long. "Graphing the Pandemic Economy," Project Syndicate, June 1, 2020.

Steinbeck, John. *The Grapes of Wrath*. New York: Viking Press, 1939.

Stiglitz, J. E., Jayadev, A., and Prabhala, A. "Patents vs. the Pandemic," Project Syndicate, April 23, 2020.

Strackey, John. *Contemporary Capitalism*, New York: Random House, 1956.

Thompson, Clive. "How 19th Century Scientists Predicted Global Warming," JSTOR.org, December 17, 2019.

Tobino, Mario. *The Mad Women of Magliano*, Verschoyle, 1954. *Le libere donne di Magliano*. Firenze: Vallecchi, 1953.

Tobino, Mario. *Gli ultimi giorni di Magliano*, Milano: Mondadori, 1982.

Todorov, Tzvetan. *Benjamin Constant. La passion démocratique*, Paris: Hachette Littératures, 1997.

Voltaire. *Candide, ou L'Optimisme*, Geneve: Cramer, Marc-Michel Rey, Jean Nourse, Lambert, and others, 1759.

Wilson, Edward O. *Consilience*. Little, Brown and Company, 1998.

Wright, Ronald. *A Short History of Progress*, Toronto: House of Anansi Press, 2004.

Zaretsky Robert. "Montaigne Fled the Plague, and Found Himself," *New York Times*, June 28, 2020.

ABOUT THE TYPE

The text is set in Dante, a typeface designed by Giovanni Mardersteig. Conceived as a private type for the Officina Bodoni in Verona, Italy, Dante was originally cut only for hand composition by Charles Malin, the famous Parisian punch cutter, between 1946 and 1952. Its first use was in an edition of Boccaccio's *Trattatello in Laude di Dante* that appeared in 1955.

OUR PHILOSOPHY

We believe that life writing is essential to living; that writing life is a privilege, right, and responsibility; that written words captivate the atmosphere of lived experience; that there are as many styles of life writing as there are lives. We are zealous preservers of memory and legacy. More than recollection of ancestors and origins, preservation is pre-serving: a proactive form of service for family, community, and posterity. Our mission is to create narratives that enlighten, entertain, and inspire while preserving stories that are vital to life.

bioGraphbook.com

ABOUT THE AUTHOR

Professor Formica is the Founder of the International Entrepreneurship Academy and a Senior Research Fellow of the Innovation Value Institute at Maynooth University in Ireland. In June 2017, Professor Formica received The Innovation Luminary Award from the Open Innovation Science and Policy Group under the aegis of the European Union for his work on modern innovation policy. His recent publications include *The Role of Creative Ignorance: Portraits of Path Finders and Path Creators, Grand Transformation Towards an Entrepreneurial Economy: Exploring the Void,* and *Econaissance: The Reimagined School and the Culture of Entrepreneurialism.*

www.ingramcontent.com/pod-product-compliance
Lightning Source LLC
La Vergne TN
LVHW020047110826
845155LV00029B/670